"Michael Hardin's knowledge of history, culture, biblical tradition and Christian faith is immense. He uses it all to provide what is so lacking, that is, someone to interpret (1 Cor 14:27) all that has been and is being said. Like his mentor (Girard), once a person reads Hardin, you can't unread him. This book is no exception. For those who have become disillusioned with fundamentalist expressions of the Christian faith (religion—both progressive or conservative) this book will help you understand why you just couldn't do it any longer, and it provides for you a hopeful, joyful path forward that is faithful to the way of Jesus."

—**DOUG KLASSEN,** Executive Minister, Mennonite Church Canada

"Michael Hardin has done it again. His book *The Jesus Driven Life* was a major shift in my theology: how I understood and interpreted scripture. Michael's new book, *Liberating the Gospel from Christian Myth* has done the same once more, by driving home the truth that all doctrine must be seen through the light of the gospel and understood through the streams of either religion or revelation. This book is written in a way that allows a younger believer to grasp and understand it, while a seasoned theologian will receive fresh light and truth from it. Written with a kind simplicity but fused with Michael's scholarly mind and wit, it is a must read for every Christ-follower's journey. I want to encourage every pastor and leader to get a copy, devour it, and then give copies to everyone you are leading. Recommend it to every believer who desires understanding and wants a solid grounding in a Christ-focused and centered theology."

—**JAMIE ENGLEHART,** Overseer, CIM Network

"Michael Hardin is, and has been, a gift of God to me for over a decade. I am privileged and blessed to have been both a friend and 'student' of his during that time. I believe he is one of the most significant, clear-thinking, ground-breaking, pioneering theological minds and voices alive today in the body of Christ. I am approaching my fiftieth year of practicing to be a follower of Jesus. I have literally read thousands of Christian books in that time—both devotional and scholarly—from the Patristic Fathers to modern authors. If I was discipling a would-be follower of Jesus today, *on day-one* I would give that person two books: a Bible and Michael Hardin's *Liberating the Gospel from Christian Myth*. That is how valuable I believe this primer is. I wish it could be in the hands of every human who calls Jesus of Nazareth Lord, or who is considering so, and who is serious about being conformed to his image and way."

—**STEPHEN R. CROSBY,** Stephanos Ministries

"This is the kind of book I have been waiting for someone to write. A book that exposes the painful distortions of the gospel and of God present within American Christianity while offering a gentle invitation to come across to the worship of a God whose love and generosity do not require violence and bloodshed or end in brutal retributive punishments. One of these days the theological world will 'discover' Michael Hardin and be better for it."

—**JOHN E. PHELAN,** Emeritus Professor, North Park Theological Seminary

# Liberating the Gospel from Christian Myth

# Liberating the Gospel from Christian Myth

## God Concepts and the Father of Jesus in Holy Scripture

MICHAEL HARDIN

*Foreword by Duane Armitage*

CASCADE *Books* • Eugene, Oregon

LIBERATING THE GOSPEL FROM CHRISTIAN MYTH
God Concepts and the Father of Jesus in Holy Scripture

Copyright © 2025 Michael Hardin. All rights reserved. Except for brief quotations in critical publications or reviews, no part of this book may be reproduced in any manner without prior written permission from the publisher. Write: Permissions, Wipf and Stock Publishers, 199 W. 8th Ave., Suite 3, Eugene, OR 97401.

Cascade Books
An Imprint of Wipf and Stock Publishers
199 W. 8th Ave., Suite 3
Eugene, OR 97401

www.wipfandstock.com

PAPERBACK ISBN: 979-8-3852-4112-5
HARDCOVER ISBN: 979-8-3852-4113-2
EBOOK ISBN: 979-8-3852-4114-9

*Cataloguing-in-Publication data:*

Names: Hardin, Michael, author. | Armitage, Duane, 1982–, foreword.

Title: Liberating the gospel from christian myth : God concepts and the father of Jesus in holy scripture / Michael Hardin ; foreword by Duane Armitage.

Description: Eugene, OR : Cascade Books, 2025 | Includes bibliographical references.

Identifiers: ISBN 979-8-3852-4112-5 (paperback) | ISBN 979-8-3852-4113-2 (hardcover) | ISBN 979-8-3852-4114-9 (ebook)

Subjects: LCSH: Bible.—Gospels—Criticism, interpretation, etc.

Classification: BV3790 .H37 2025 (paperback) | BV3790 (ebook)

06/20/25

This little book is dedicated to
Tommy Kleyn, Greg Vadala, Karsten Johnson, and Keith Hayes
For their unwavering support and friendship
and to
Cheryl Sletten-Hardin
For her love, gentleness, wisdom and chocolate chip cookies
Semper lucem invenias in evangelio Iesu Christi

# Contents

*Foreword by Duane Armitage* — xi
*Preface* — xvii
1. Religion — 1
2. Revelation — 19
3. God and the Bible — 42
4. The Devil — 65
5. Reframing Christian Doctrine — 90

*Bibliography* — 107

# Foreword

I first met Michael Hardin in 2017, a meeting that would become one of the most profound days of both my academic and spiritual life. At that time, I was in the midst of writing a book on René Girard and philosophy—a thinker whose insights had, like for Michael, reshaped me on a philosophical, theological, and existential level. I had recently encountered several of Michael's works, knowing that he had not only studied under Girard but also was a personal friend of Girard. Hoping for a phone conversation, I reached out, eager to discuss his insights. To my surprise and gratitude, Michael warmly invited me to visit him at his home.

Michael greeted me at the door, bearing an uncanny resemblance to Jeff Bridges's character "The Dude" from *The Big Lebowski*[1]—that is, if "The Dude" had a PhD! Michael's relaxed demeanor, coupled with a booming laugh, radiated a confidence and openness that immediately set the stage for what would become a time of great conversation, and, for me, conversion. Now, walking into Michael's house was like stepping into a vast library—an entire floor of his home is, in fact, a library, and one that is filled with any and every imaginable book related to philosophy, religion, theology, literature, etc.

Throughout the day, Michael and I spent hours discussing mimetic theory, a subject of which he clearly was a master, having written extensively and known Rene Girard himself. Yet, what struck me about Michael, aside mastery of Girard's ideas, was his command of Greek and Latin, as well as biblical studies, theology, philosophy, and history. It was as if no area of thought was beyond his grasp or irrelevant to the conversation. Furthermore, his kindness, warmth, and incredible humor were so very apparent

---

1 Directed by Joel Coen; Universal City, CA: Gramercy Pictures, 1998.

to me in our exchanges, making it clear that Michael was not just a scholar, but a true polymath with a heart to match his intellect.

But what struck me most about Michael was his ability to remain objective on topics that often elicit severely entrenched biases, especially among academics and theologians. Our conversations touched on everything from politics and philosophy to theology and mimetic theory, as well as the state of academia itself. It was clear that Michael's insights were not bound by the usual constraints; he was able to engage with controversial and complex issues without falling into the traps of partisanship or dogma, all the while remaining passionate, enthusiastic, and most importantly, kind.

His, again unique objectivity was evident to me already in his social media presence, where he has a remarkable following. His ability to distill profound and intricate ideas for both lay and academic audiences has resulted in a series of books, aptly titled *What the Facebook?*,[2] where he unpacks contemporary issues and timeless questions with equal clarity, and again, charity. To successfully bridge the gap between popular and scholarly discourse requires a command of the material that most academics simply do not possess. Michael's talent for doing this speaks not just to his knowledge, but to his vocation; a calling that goes beyond the typical role of a scholar. Nevertheless, to be able to do all of this on social media requires, again, incredible objectivity, as well as significant courage. That is, Michael is not afraid to say what he believes to be true and what he has committed himself to, even if that means saying what (for the moment at least) could be seen as unpopular. It is for all of these reasons and more, as I will explain, that I am deeply honored to write this foreword for Michael and, even more so, to count Michael as a friend.

Now, Michael's significant contributions to mimetic theory stand out to me in particular. His approach, while of course deeply rooted in Girard, brings fresh perspectives that illuminate the complexities of human desire, rivalry, and violence in ways that resonate across different audiences. His ability to appeal to both scholars and everyday readers is not just a rare gift; it is an almost impossible task that Michael embraces with humility and enthusiasm. Michael's larger-than-life personality, combined with his intellectual rigor and ability to engage diverse audiences, make him a figure who is so unique in today's academic and theological landscape.

As I visited with Michael, our discussions, much like Michael's writings, were not limited to intellectual and academic matters; they also

---

2 Self-published, 2014–16.

# Foreword

ventured into deeply spiritual territory. We spoke at length about prayer, the nature of faith, and the atonement of Christ. Michael approached these topics with the same rigor and openness that he brought to his scholarly work, yet there was a profound reverence and joy in the way he spoke about spiritual issues. Unlike many academics, whose familiarity with such subjects can often seem abstract or detached, Michael's passion and apparent and clear firsthand knowledge shone through. His understanding was not merely theoretical, but wildly experiential—a kind of knowledge born from living and believing the very ideas he discussed.

When Michael spoke of Jesus, he was clearly not speaking of an abstraction or a figure from faith or history. Rather, he spoke with the conviction of someone sharing about a close friend, someone whom he knew intimately and personally. In other words, when Michael spoke of, and still now speaks of Christ, he speaks of someone he knows, and of whom he continually encounters in a deep and transformative way. For me, Michael's words carried the weight of a lived faith and a relationship that was as real to him as any human friendship. This was perhaps the most powerful aspect of our conversations: witnessing a scholar whose scholarship was not detached from his faith, but deeply intertwined with his lived experience of knowing God. Any scholar who knows or who reads Michael Hardin cannot help but want to emulate him.

As to some of Michael's most powerful contributions to mimetic theory and to Christianity and Christian thinking as a whole: first and foremost, as alluded to above, these contributions lie in his ability to navigate the delicate balance between right- and left-wing interpretations—not just politically, but also philosophically and theologically. Indeed, Michael transcends any and every label. In a landscape often defined by rigid camps and ideological divisions, Michael is a free and genuine thinker, impossible to categorize. His thought resists easy classification, and that very quality is what makes his work so profound and vital particularly in 2024, where every idea is immediately labelled as right or left.

An area particularly significant for me in Michael's work, which is continued and deepened significantly in this book, is the Atonement. In this book, Michael continues to masterfully illuminate how much of Christian history has been dominated by, as he puts it, "economies of exchange," that lock us into a conception of God as "Janus-faced"—appearing both loving and wrathful. He shows how these interpretations serve to reduce the divine to a transactional deity. This book in particular seeks to develop and deepen a language to free the atonement from this limiting framework, revealing a deeper, more radical understanding of divine love that transcends such economies of exchange. His approach, in particular, manages to bring a fresh perspective to the nature of God, breaking away from conceptions that perpetuate cycles of guilt, retribution, and sacrificial logic, in a way that I can think of no other book doing.

Interestingly, alongside Michael Hardin's rare gift for engaging with people from all walks of life—whether seasoned academics, curious laypersons, or spiritual seekers—he also possesses a remarkable and, at times, unsettling ability to challenge, confront, and even *offend* a wide range of audiences. In this, Michael embodies what Kierkegaard famously identified as the "offense" at the heart of the Gospel: that sacred capacity to shake us out of complacency, to awaken us to truths we might otherwise resist. Just as Socrates acted as a gadfly to the city of Athens, Michael's words and ideas stir the minds and hearts of his readers, urging them to see and hear with fresh eyes and ears. Make no mistake, this book will challenge its reader.

This book, true to Michael's spirit, does not offer comfortable platitudes or neatly packaged answers. Instead, it is jam-packed with insights that pierce to the heart of some of the most ingrained assumptions in Christian thought—from critiques of biblical inerrancy and penal substitution to the pervasive sacrificial ways of thinking that have seeped into unreflective, everyday theology, to name a few. This book demands nothing less than multiple, careful readings; for me personally, it is a book I will return to and study again and again.

I assure you that it is not in any way hyperbole to say that this book calls for nothing short of a revolutionary reorientation of Christian thought—a return to the core message of the Gospel by disentangling it from the often rigid structures of doctrine. That is, here Michael argues that a fundamental error, which took root in early Christianity, was the shift from trust to correct doctrine, which in turn birthed and enabled the prioritizing of *gnosis* over *pistis*. As Michael writes, "I would like to single out a basic, primary, fundamental mistake that early Christianity made, and this can be seen in the shift away from 'trust' to 'correct doctrine.' This move is known as 'Gnosticism,' the belief that correct knowledge saves us. Early Christian gnostics proliferated like rabbits in the second century."

However, for Michael, Gnosticism is not a relic of the past, but a persistent heresy, tempting each generation to substitute intellectual assent for the radical trust at the heart of the Gospel. A primary preoccupation of

## Foreword

this book is thus to reveal and deconstruct the latent and hidden forms of Gnosticism in contemporary Christian thinking. I therefore place Michael's methodology, in this book at least, like Heidegger, Riceour, and even Nietzsche, as deeply rooted in a form of "suspicious hermeneutics."

In a powerful passage, he reflects, "I have never left the great Christian doctrines, but I have learned that these doctrines need to be seen in the light of the Gospel rather than the other way around." Here, Michael calls for a faith that is not subordinate to doctrine but one that transforms doctrine—allowing trust in God, rather than intellectual adherence, to shape Christian life. As he explains, "The way of trust is so very different. Knowledge that arises from the trust relation established in the gospel retains its focus on that which makes the Good News good news indeed, namely that the Father is not like any of our gods." Michael's critique is as daring as it is necessary, in that it challenges us to reclaim the gospel's core relational message and abandon notions of divinity, justice, and community that have been distorted by a rigid *Theoria*, a distorted *Gnosis*.

The heart of this book lies in how doctrine is lived out in human relationships, and Michael seamlessly connects theological understanding with human transformation. As he writes, "The entire point of this little book is to show how intimately theology and human relations are intertwined." In his vision, doctrine is not a set of propositions, but rather a language that communicates our faith through actions. Again, in Michael's words, "Doctrine matters because doctrine is the intellectual linguistic way you communicate why you behave the way you do. Your actions show your faith and your language about God in relation to these matters."

Laid out carefully in this book then, in a way that is for me unprecedented, is an intermingling of academic rigor and a call to faith and action. Michael's book here then is not simply an invitation to do theology, but rather to engage in what the church fathers understood to be primary theological discourse, *theologia* proper, which is to live and imitate Jesus Christ in an act of true "spiritual worship" (Rom 12:1). As Michael writes, "The gospel does not present us with a set of laws to obey; it gives us a person to willingly imitate." This is a gospel centered on learning to suffer without retaliation, to forgive instead of demanding justice, and to walk the path of the cross—not as a masochistic exercise, but as a radical embodiment of trust in God's love and mercy.

In sum, what Michael Hardin provides in this book is a model for reinterpreting doctrine in light of trust rather than as a pursuit of theoretical knowledge. By doing so, he offers a theology that doesn't just speak to our minds but challenges our entire way of being. It is a book that demands more than one reading, and for me, it will be a companion for years to come—a book to study, wrestle with, and let transform my faith.

In every book Michael Hardin writes, I find myself thinking, "This must be his best work." And each time, he somehow surpasses himself, transversing deeper into the heart of the gospel, human culture, anthropology, and mimetic theory. This book is no exception. In it, he solidifies and expands upon his most essential insights, unearthing the true gospel and bringing to light the manifold ways in which the gospel is distorted. As noted above, I see Michael's work as largely a project in the tradition of the hermeneutics of suspicion; indeed, it was Martin Luther who first sought to deconstruct Christianity's unholy marriage to theoretical thinking, what Luther called a "theology of glory," in favor of a "theology of the cross," that is, a theology that put faith in the living God in Christ at the center. I see Michael's work as a timely and much needed reappropriation of Luther's initial deconstructive project.

Every page in this book challenges assumptions, uncovers blind spots, and compels a reevaluation of what it truly means to follow Christ. This is a book that will remain by my side, a text to return to repeatedly, as it continues to challenge and deepen my understanding. With this work, Michael Hardin once again demonstrates why he is one of the most compelling and necessary voices in contemporary theology.

DUANE ARMITAGE
Professor of Philosophy
University of Scranton
Scranton, Pennsylvania

# Preface

This little book is intended to be read with a view to the care of the soul. In the almost fifty years I have been engaged with Christian theology, church history, and biblical studies, I have found that books that address the human condition without rose-colored glasses or utopian dreams, those works that address the real questions that plague the Christian mind, to be those works that have an eye on the well-being of the Christian. It has been pointed out that doctrine and doctor share a common denominator, which means that doctrine which does not bring healing in its wake is not Christian doctrine.

We exist in a period of what has been called deconstruction and there are numerous books for and against such an approach. This book involves deconstruction, as does all theology. I cannot think of a theological book I have ever read that does not involve a change in thinking and the best books are those that left splinters in my mind. This book involves a serious amount of rebuilding, though inasmuch as it seeks to acknowledge the insights of the classic Christian doctrines, it is at the same time learning how to approach them from within the new perspective given in the gospel of Jesus Christ. This book brings to the forefront of my theological work the most significant conclusions that I have come to.

I have, to the very best of my ability, written this book for the regular person that has no theological training but is interested in how to retain the best parts of their faith tradition, or learn how to reframe them so that they bring clarity and healing instead of obscurity and fear. Any time I felt my writing becoming too academic I sought to include definitions. I wish to be as clear and understandable as possible, but having to overcome two thousand years of encrustation, Christian doctrine sometimes needs a sledgehammer taken to it. This is my eleventh book, and it continues to build on my previous work. Interested readers may wish to follow this by reading *The Jesus Driven Life: Reconnecting Humanity with Jesus* (2013) or *Knowing God: Consumer Christianity and the Gospel of Jesus* (2020).

A word about fear: The Christian religion has always had a component of fear built into it. No doubt one can go to just about any author and find hope, but in most cases it is hope tinged with fear. Some go to heaven, and some go to hell. What is your lot? Who knows? And so, fear lingers. Some fear examining the theology they were given from the pulpit or Bible College they attended because they are frozen, afraid to make a move out of concern they will be leaving "the faith delivered once for all to the saints" (Jude 1:3).

Do not fear. The perfect love of God in the gospel of Jesus Christ shed abroad in our hearts by the Holy Spirit casts out all fear. Like an exorcist casting out the demonic, the Gospel comes into our lives and kicks out fear. Boots it away, permanently. Gone! Poof! There is nothing to fear in the gospel and there is nothing to fear from the God of the Gospel.

Your challenge as you read this is to ask what makes more sense, the view proposed here or the views you have heard from the Fundamentalist-Evangelical churches. I have no doubt there will be fierce critics of this little book, but I know why they are afraid. They are terrified of grace. They cower before love. They need an angry God in order to justify their own anger. On the other hand, to those who are leaving or have left Protestantism behind, who are weary of the constant soul searching to determine one's value or worth, to those who have had mental breakdowns because of the preaching of an angry God who will roast them on a spit over hell's flames, this book offers solace and a balm for the mind and soul.

A lot in my life has changed since the publication of my last book. In fact, one could say I have begun a totally new journey. I met and married a true companion in whose life I see the goodness of the Father, the grace of Jesus, and the passion of the Spirit. I moved from Lancaster, Pennsylvania, to Minneapolis, Minnesota. As I enter the final season of my life, I find myself evermore interested in seeing Christianity flourish. I spend my days reading, pondering, meditating and praying, sprinkled with conversations that help me to go from one new stepping to another as I cross the river of my own theological life.

Duane Armitage has been a friend of mine for many years and I welcome his effusive foreword. As a professor of philosophy, he brings to the table abundant knowledge and sharp critical skills. He is one of the few who has openly shared with me that the path I have been taking these many

# Preface

years is a beneficial one that seems to answer a lot of questions that have puzzled many great minds. Thank you, Duane, for your willingness to jump in the fray with me.

I also wish to thank my "students," who are really more like co-sojourners with me on this path of discovery. An especial thanks to Tommy Kleyn who has stood by me with support for my soul, my mind and my life.

Finally, I gratefully acknowledge that I am changing. My students see it as do others in my life and on my social media platforms. I am not as feisty as I used to be and I have walked away from arguing with others (well, OK, I have turned the burner from high to simmer). I know why this is so. These changes are due to Cheryl Sletten-Hardin, my beautiful and wonderful wife whose wisdom and common sense are the rod and staff that comfort me. It is to her that this book is dedicated. I love you, sweetheart.

Michael Hardin
Minneapolis, 2024

# 1

# Religion

I know you. I know why you picked up this book. I know your faith struggles. I know how hard it is to make sense of the world today. More so, I know how difficult it is to make sense of the Bible today. There are so many voices saying so many different things. It is little wonder so many have thrown up their hands when it comes to the Bible, or why so many others have turned to some sort of subjective interpretation. Some folks even claim they don't need to study because the Holy Spirit tells them what the Bible means. No matter how one slices or dices it, inevitably all of these interpretations can be traced to a few common presuppositions.

These presuppositions are the problem, and we will be examining them all throughout this book. Our problem with theology is misplaced if we claim it is too hard or academic. It is also misplaced if we view theology simply as "the words of man" (or human discourse). Christian theology, at its best, is simply the repetition of the gospel in language that can be understood by the people. This language engages the questions and conundrums of the time and place at which this gospel is announced, but it is not ruled by these questions, for one thing the gospel exposes is how we often ask the wrong questions. When we do so we get the wrong answers.

Now for centuries, and especially this past several decades, too many have assumed the legitimacy of the questions but have also despised the theological solutions proposed to deal with them. For example, how are we to relate everything Jesus says about his Father with everything that is said in the Jewish Scriptures? Some have simply tossed out the Older Testament while others seek to find a one-to-one correspondence. How does one deal with the question of an angry God? This question is asked and answered in the gospel, but it is not answered in the way we want. As we shall see, the gospel gives us a new way of thinking that has us looking at both our questions and their purported solutions.

The problem lies not so much in *what* we think as in *how* we think. How we think influences what we think. How we think can either limit us or open us up. Sadly, for many, all they can see is what they think, and so they accept or reject certain doctrines but have no idea that how they think determines that which is accepted or rejected. For example, if one reads the Bible literally, one must make each verse of the Bible "fit" with every other verse. Or one can say that there is no revelation of God in the Bible and pick and choose which biblical verses one uses to live by.

Either way, what the Bible is doing as a collection of texts is missed.

There is a way to read the Bible that is not done in willful ignorance or religious pride. There is a way to come to the Bible and see the big picture without getting all bogged down in useless speculative arguments. One of the more interesting things about the Bible is how it continually engenders new insights into the human condition. The influence of the Bible on human culture has been great. While the Bible gets blamed for a lot of things, it has also been of great benefit to humanity. The Bible is not the problem; the issue has to do with its interpreters who, as I mentioned, come to the biblical text assuming they know what words like God, sin, or redemption mean. We fail to see that one of the things the Bible does is to redefine so many of these terms, and in doing so it changes the way we think about things.

Frustratingly, too many so-called well-meaning Christians, especially out there on social media, have taken it upon themselves to correct everyone that disagrees with them. Everyone is an expert on social media if they have a concordance and a dictionary. Both you and I have seen some wild and crazy speculation on biblical texts and the way they are interpreted. The extreme, outlandish posts and comments can be easily recognized. But there are many more subtle interpretations on offer that "seem" or "feel" like they could be legitimate, but on closer inspection contain some of the hidden assumptions we mentioned earlier. For someone familiar with the original languages and ancient history it is easy to spot these delusional comments, but what is the regular working person to do? They have not had the opportunity to spend years or decades studying.

## Religion

Over the past thirty years, but especially in the last fifteen, there has taken place a major shift in American Protestant Christianity. People, like yourself, have left organized religion behind and no longer attend a church, yet find themselves still on a spiritual-theological journey. They seek to understand what it is they believe, even if that belief has been in a process of (so-called) deconstruction. These same people still have a love for Jesus and a robust appreciation of the Bible but find themselves as sheep without a shepherd. They want to believe that the divine is benevolent. They want to believe that goodness and grace was manifested in Jesus, yet they need a way to connect their hopes and questions either back to Scripture or to the Christian tradition.

In this book we will examine the roadblocks put before the average believer by both culture and church. Ultimately, we will find that these roadblocks are paper thin, but when we first hit them, they are solid as concrete. It takes some time and effort to transform them from the paper tiger doctrines that used to frighten us.

While this book is aimed at those who have abandoned the Fundamentalist and Evangelical viewpoint and who still love Jesus and appreciate the Bible, who have become part of the Nones and Dones, what is said will apply also to the progressive liberal Protestant tradition in America. Inasmuch as I think that movement has had its day and is becoming but a shadow of its former self, I do not feel the need to further dismantle the dysfunctional thinking of that part of Christendom. There is a liberal form of fundamentalism. It differs in that the early twentieth-century fundamentalists were concerned to affirm the "classic" doctrines of Christianity (those especially found in the Nicene Creed). Fundamentalists became mesmerized over words and required belief in a very specific way: it was their interpretation that was God's word as much as "the Bible was God's word." There was no distinction to be made between what they said and what the Bible said.

Liberal Protestant Christianity has its shibboleths as well. Phrases, slogans, worldviews, and theories that each in their own way form that which must be believed. These are not doctrinal, but they are social and political. In this way of thinking language is used fetishistically. Just as for the Conservative, so too for the Liberal Progressive, exact words matter. Say the wrong thing and you will get the boot.

Rather my focus in this little book is on those who still believe that there is value to be derived from the Bible and from the larger Christian tradition. Like you, I believe that the Bible matters, and like you, I believe that God has been completely revealed in the person, life and teaching of Jesus of Nazareth. My liberal colleagues have written off Scripture, and worse, they have tossed out the categories by which we are to understand this revelation. Doctrines like the Trinity, the deity of Jesus, and his resurrection from the grave have been called into question. Jesus has been reduced in this tradition to a social prophet. It is true, Jesus is a social prophet. But he is also far more than that.

My conservative friends are still reading their Bibles in the dark with sunglasses on. Jesus gets reduced in this tradition to a pawn in some sick divine game. I find it almost impossible to have discussions with them anymore. Their minds are like cement: all mixed up and permanently set. It is like talking to a subwoofer set on ten. I am thankful it is not my task to unstop their ears. I leave that kind of work to God.

Now there are five pillars of the Fundamentalist-Evangelical tradition. Each of these is necessary in one form or another to their tradition, but where all five are present we have a clear indication of the anti-gospel in all its horror. Some Evangelicals have tried to find alternative readings of some of these, but almost always end up back where they began. These Pillars are a "required" belief in:

- The inerrancy or infallibility of the Protestant Bible
- The penal substitutionary atonement
- Eternal conscious torment (Hell)
- A theology of glory
- Sacrificial thinking

Let us take each in their own order.

## PILLAR #1: THE INERRANCY OR INFALLIBILITY OF THE BIBLE

Holy Scripture has always played a significant role in the life of the church, just as the Jewish Tanakh did in Second Temple Judaism. The Apostolic writings are chock full of quotes, allusions, and references back to the more widely recognized Jewish Scriptures (it must be noted that there was not a canon of Scriptures in the time of Jesus or the early church; different groups had different canons). The Bible as a collection of the texts of those who call themselves the people of God cannot be dispensed with. The Bible is not an appendage to Christianity; the Bible is Christianity's brain and nervous system (and to extend the metaphor and anticipate where we are going, certain doctrines are the skeletal system, while ethics is the musculature).

Five hundred years ago, at the time of the Reformation, the Protestants needed an authority by which to challenge the Roman papacy and its stranglehold on doctrine and the people. Luther, Calvin, Zwingli, and the first Anabaptists all turned to the Bible. It was at this time that the Bible began to be translated into the language of the European peoples. The Bible as an authority over Rome was also welcomed by many of the princes, kings, dukes, and other royalty as a way to throw off Roman (Italian) chains and control all of life in their own territories.

One hundred years after the Reformation a war broke out in Europe. It was a specifically religious war pitting Catholic against Protestant and Protestant against Protestant. The remnants of this war have extended all the way into the late twentieth century in the Troubles in Ireland. From 1618–48, the Thirty Years War decimated Europe. Millions of soldiers died, and that's discounting collateral damage. Over the next one hundred years the Bible began to be devalued and, in its place, the human mind, or reason, reigned as the supreme authority.

It was during this time, as critical approaches to the Bible were developed (mid to late seventeenth century), that some felt the need to "prove" that the Bible was not a collection of human religious texts but was in fact God's very word. While infallibility had been attributed to the biblical writings for centuries, now a term was invented: *inerrancy*. The term meant that God himself dictated every word found in the original Hebrew and Greek manuscripts. The Bible even declared itself to be God's very word as in 2 Tim 3:16 (my translation): "All scripture is inspired by God . . ." For instance, it was at this time that the first critical scholars began to question the truth of the Gospels. Why did the cleansing of the temple take place at the end of Jesus's ministry in Matthew, Mark, and Luke (the Synoptic Gospels) while in the Gospel of John this takes place at the very beginning of Jesus's ministry? Or does any letter purported to have been written by Paul come from Paul? The Pastorals (1 and 2 Timothy and Titus) were quite different from Paul's other letters so perhaps they were pseudonymous, that is, composed in Paul's name, a widely accepted practice in ancient times.

At any rate, the Protestant orthodox tradition reacted quite harshly insisting that if the Bible said it, it meant what it said and was to be taken literally. End of story. The battle lines were drawn, and as Christianity moved into the eighteenth and nineteenth centuries the *battle for the Bible* began. How was one to reconcile all the contradictions and alleged errors in the Bible with the theory that if God is perfect and God wrote the Bible then the Bible is perfect? The attempts to reconcile all these issues bordered on the ludicrous at times, with solutions stretching the imagination and torturing the mind. Nevertheless, Protestant Orthodoxy held this line and continues to do so until this day. Their approach to the Bible is fraught with special pleading and irrational defenses.

Over time, the view that God wrote the Bible or that everything it says about God is infallible and must be believed has come crashing down, despite the Protestant tradition's attempt to uphold it. In the second half of the twentieth century the Bible slipped the bonds of the churches and entered the academy, and departments of religion were born. They studied the Bible simply as an ancient document, as literature, and applied the same criteria to studying Scripture as was applied to all other literature. Thus, slowly, to the great consternation of the orthodox Protestant tradition, the Bible began to fade from influence and become pretty much regarded as a relic. Have a family Bible, record everybody's names in it, but don't pay it much attention after that.

Now, for our purposes, this first pillar, this perfectionist view of the Bible, requires one to avoid all of the hard questions that have been put to the Bible for the past four hundred years. The Protestant tradition really never secured the doctrine of the authority of Scripture. Part of this lies in the fact that the earliest Reformers (1500–60) did not share the same view of the Bible. Martin Luther, John Calvin, and the Anabaptists all held differing understandings of the authority of Scripture. There never was a unified view until the rise of Evangelicalism in the mid-twentieth century. Since that time this theory of the Bible has infiltrated all manner of Protestant traditions, and to their detriment.

Here is the problem: the Bible appears to contradict itself all over the place. There are different creation stories. Tales are told where in one version God is the antagonist, but the exact same story in another writer has the satan as the antagonist. There are confused and confusing genealogies. Acts and the Pauline letters contradict each other, and the Gospel of John is contradicted by the Synoptic Gospels. The inerrancy viewpoint requires that one harmonize these "apparent" contradictions, but this requires a twisting of the text like taffy. Sure, it might be "a solution" but does it have merit? Very rarely. More often than not, so-called harmonizations of Scripture are smoke and mirrors, taking away with one hand what they give with the other. These proposed solutions never seem to work on an intellectual level.

But, and this is my point, inerrancy is not a theory of the authority of Scripture. It is an interpretation disguised as a theory. This "theory" assumes no errors or contradictions, so any that are found are only apparent in the liberal interpretive mind. The theory says to trust the theory for the theory can be trusted, resulting in a circular logic, the kind of logic found in authoritarian cults the world over. Inerrancy is not a theory of the authority of scripture, it is a hermeneutic, a method for interpreting the Bible.

Inerrancy has been tested as a hypothesis and found lacking.

# PILLAR #2: THE PENAL SUBSTITUTIONARY THEORY OF THE ATONEMENT (PSA)

Jesus died and paid the price for my sins by taking the just punishment of God's wrath against sin in my place. This, in a nutshell is PSA, or the Penal Substitutionary Theory of Atonement. It is an explanation of why Jesus died and what his death accomplished. It is preached around the world by the Fundamentalist-Evangelical church, and *It. Is. A. Lie.* In fact, it is the perfect perversion of the gospel, so subtle and so deceptive that it is easily swallowed whole by the masses. Now there is a reason for this naivete on the part of the many and we shall have to discuss this later. For now, all one needs to know is this: in this view of Jesus's death, God (presumably the Father) doesn't save us from an eternal damnation. No, God saves us from God's holy and righteous self. PSA is the story of how an angry God saved us from the divine dark side.

The Protestant orthodox tradition has misread biblical texts by the hundreds and created an understanding of Jesus's death that boggles the mind. Why would a God create a hell in the first place? Why would a holy God commit such crimes as killing humans and sanctioning the death of children? Why would this God substitute his only beloved Son for us and infinitely torture this Son? What kind of a god is this? Our orthodox friends would tell us that we must hold God's attributes in tension but as I said in my book *The Jesus Driven Life* (2013), to define God as a series of nouns and adjectives and call them attributes, all required to square with one another, is to create a Frankenstein god made up of many dead parts. PSA pits the

Father against the Son, does not even involve the Holy Spirit, and frankly makes the Father out to be someone who should be committed, arrested, or put out to pasture.

We have rightfully rejected this.

First, this doctrine has a history, and its origins can be located in the sixteenth-century theology of John Calvin. It is true that Calvin, trained as a lawyer, had a penal view of the death of Jesus. It is also true that later Calvinism would distort Calvin's view on this. Calvin at least was seeking to protect God's grace in his theology, with salvation being above all from the kindness of God. However, Calvin's immediate followers in Geneva would turn his theological frame into a binary dualism of elect and non-elect and proceed to work out all of the legalities of the atoning process and eschatology (the way things end up), including the need for payment and/or punishment.

Second, this understanding of Jesus's death sounds suspiciously like that of ancient myth and ritual where human sacrifice was practiced, only now this practice is played out between the Father and the Son. We shall have cause to critique this distortion of the death of Jesus, but here we must be careful not to simply run to another theory like Christ the Victor (Christus Victor, the dominant view of the death of Jesus for the first 1,100 years), or to the Moral Theory (where Jesus's death demonstrates the love of the Father), for even here there are elements that, when added to the gospel, create distortions (Origen would be a good example with his view of the redemption of the satan).

Third, the PSA view of the atonement opens the floodgates for justified abuse. If God can do it so can we. I will show you that there is an intimate connection in the gospel between our view of the death of Jesus (reconciliation), our understanding of what constitutes Christian or Jesus-like behavior (ethics) and our view of how it all works out in the end (eschatology). If God functions like a dry drunk and we also are justified in our dualistic behavior, hating this one, loving that one, etc., we are all in trouble. But we now recognize the poison of this view and have moved on.

## PILLAR #3: ETERNAL CONSCIOUS TORMENT (ECT)

Hell? Hell no! We have too long lived in the medieval shadow of Dante's Inferno. Most of us were taught that to reject whatever the preacher was telling us would inevitably get us a one-way ticket to the hottest, nastiest place in all of creation, where the dead are consciously alive and aware as their flesh burns and worms eat their charred bodies, where there is no escape from the flames of God's wrath against sin. And we *did not* want to end up there. I remember as a child living in daily fear of this eventual possibility. As a teenager I grew more afraid, and demons and hell and the frightening aspect of being possessed by the devil were only intensified by the horrid and haunting images of artists' depictions of hell.

Why would God create such a place? Because he needed a dumping ground for all those who would reject his message. God is so holy, his wrath knowing no bounds of time or space, that he must, is indeed obligated to char broil everyone who disobeys him. Back in 2012 I had the pleasure of working with director Kevin Miller on his film *Hellbound?* In my opinion it is still a wonderful teaching tool for those who are just beginning to question this infernal doctrine. Alternatives which include annihilation seem more compassionate, and of course universal salvation seems the best of all possible outcomes. But the Bible speaks of all three as options. Which one is true?

The understanding of the afterlife as a jail cell or a place of punishment has long tormented the souls of the faithful, particularly when a loved one dies who did not conform to the church's teaching. Little wonder then that purgatory, which limits punishment in both scope and duration, is a preferable alternative and perhaps the Roman Catholic tradition has something to contribute here.

The doctrine of ECT has been used by the Christian churches quite effectively as a tool to keep the people in fear and the church in business. However, at the same time that PSA was being challenged, it is also the case that in the eighteenth and nineteenth centuries, the notion of ECT was also put to the test. As the Enlightenment progressed it became apparent that ECT was seen not as justice but injustice, and so it is little wonder we find writers from this period making the case for universal salvation.

We have left behind the concept of ECT for a variety of reasons. My primary reason for abandoning it is its element of fear. It seems to me that a truly loving God, like a truly loving parent, would not ever think about some sort of malicious punishment for mistakes, errors, or even disobedience. Now I also have good grounds for leaving this behind if I can show there is a trajectory in the Bible which also leaves ECT behind.

## PILLAR #4: A THEOLOGY OF GLORY

This phrase may sound odd at first. I am using it in the same way Martin Luther did in his 1518 Heidelberg Disputation. A theology of glory is juxtaposed with a theology of the cross. A theology of glory is one where success, fame, power, wealth, and fortune are sure signs that God is favorable toward a person. From the perspective of a theology of glory, a person who is poor, homeless, diseased, or broken is obviously not being favored or blessed by God. Luther challenged this. He argued that a church which had great wealth, power, esteem, and fortune was turning to a theology of glory to justify the material satisfactions of life. He also contended that this was false.

When I teach my students the difference between a theology of glory and a theology of the cross, I turn them to the viewpoint of the book of Deuteronomy (or what is called the Deuteronomic hermeneutic). This approach in Torah states the those who do good, those who obey the commandments of God, will be blessed. Conversely, those who disobey will be cursed. If such is the case, it is but a small leap in logic to say that people whose lives show little evidence of struggle are blessed by God while those who evince hardships must have sinned and are thus under a curse.

Today churches measure success by the number of people filling the pews and the amount of money being raised. When I was a pastor and went to pastor's conferences all the nattily dressed clergy wanted to boast of the number of baptisms or new members or building programs. Those of us sent to small, often struggling congregations had nothing to fall back upon. It was obvious we had not taken the latest church growth seminar or had failed in our attempts to get a congregation roused enough to pay for the mortgage envisioned by our inflated ego. We were failures in ministry for we had little or nothing to show for years, sometimes decades of faithful work.

A recent phenomenon related to a theology of glory can be found in the charismatic-Pentecostal tradition whereby signs and wonders, miracles superb and supreme, the showering of glory clouds and gold dust or some other silly "supernatural" sights are proof that God is indeed with us. This is insidious, for it limits the activity of the divine to the extraordinary. The natural rhythms of life, the ordinary relation, the same old day-to-day life, the chirping of birds, the breath of wind or the cleansing of rain, these were all nice, but they had nothing to do with God's activity. As we continue forward in the twenty-first century I expect, as times get troubled, more and more of this. Why?

Because people want a God who is a superhero. They want a strong God, not a weak one. They want a God who will fight for them and slay their enemies, not a God who will seek reconciliation with our enemies. When things go askew in our lives, we all, all of us, instinctively turn to God and ask for that which is out of the ordinary. I have even asked for winning lottery ticket numbers, for days to be turned back to start over, for God to punish those who hurt me. Each time I was seeking a *powerful* almighty sovereign God, one who controlled all things and could, *if* that God wanted, push a button and make everything all right. I had a boo-boo and wanted God to kiss it, make it better, and make it go away.

This kind of a God is found everywhere. In fact, the one thing all gods have in common (in henotheism) is some kind of superpower or (in monotheism) control over all things. Then the questions arise: why doesn't God answer prayers and why do bad things happen to good people and why, oh why, won't You, God, just flipping grant this one little request I am begging YOU for over and over again? Was God deaf? Did God care? Was I bad in some way? If I was, could I ever be forgiven? Or was I doomed by my mistakes to live a life of poverty, failure and regret? It was obvious according to the Christians that God was against me and not for me. I had no way to prove God was with me.

As we forge ahead, we will explore the alternative view, a theology of the Cross. For now, just as there are alternative views to inerrancy, PSA, and ECT, just be aware there is an alternative to a theology of glory.

These four pillars are cemented and held together by the ultimate theological glue. It is more powerful than you can imagine or think and is so strong that it has held these poorly conceived doctrines and their historic predecessors together for 1,900 years. This glue, or cement, or that which binds these distorted doctrines together is ancient, in fact, it is not only the oldest of them all but also produces them. One could say it is the mother of the Fundamentalist-Evangelical message if it were not the case that this glue began being applied to the Christian tradition already in the first century. It can in some cases can be found not just in the Old Testament but also in the New Testament. I call this glue sacrificial thinking.

## PILLAR #5: SACRIFICIAL THINKING

In the next chapter we shall have occasion to explore and critique sacrificial thinking, our task being to understand what it is and how it functions in our theology. If you were to ask a fish to describe water, how could they do so? In the same way, we humans are all saturated in sacrificial thought. It can be as mundane as an eye for an eye, or it can be as heinous as the sacrifice of virgins to volcano gods. It can be as simple as monetary restitution and as awful as the death penalty. In the end, all sacrificial thinking is grounded in an understanding of human relations as transactions. Sacrificial thinking permeates all of our understanding of relationships, both the human and divine relation as well as the human-to-human relation.

Sacrificial thinking is perhaps the earliest known "pattern" of thought. I give in order to receive. I subscribe to a theory of religion that places sacrificial thinking at the heart of religion. In its basics it is quite simple. Human communities suffer from innumerable conflicts. These conflicts can be resolved by everyone fighting everyone else. When this occurs the group or society is in the process of destroying itself. What is the solution to people fighting over things? Simple. Find someone to blame for all of our problems. If we can all agree that such and such a person was to blame then we can all take our collective anger out on this one, sacrifice them to the gods and voila! With our pent-up violence discharged on such a person we now have a sort of peace, and we can get about the business of restoring our family, group, or nation.

We commonly call this scapegoating, but there are nuances to this process we will need to explore in order to understand just how it is that the gospel challenges this kind of thinking at its very core. Sacrificial thinking always involves blood or death. Someone must pay and some of you have been that someone, arbitrarily selected as the one who caused the troubles, and evicted, cast off and cast out, ostracized, treated like a pariah. Do you know what I mean? Yet how many of us are willing to acknowledge our part in these dramas where we joined with the mob, the group, the majority to say, "Hey, you're right! If so-and-so was not part of us, we would be much better off!" It is easy to claim the post of scapegoat, not so easy to acknowledge our complicity in the act of scapegoating. Sacrificial thinking justifies any and all violence as legitimate as long as it is our own righteous indignation and demand for justice and is unjustified when it comes from another.

With these five pillars, or four pillars and the sacrificial logic that holds them together, we have the basis for the message that has now gone global. God wrote a perfect book, sent his Son to die a death experiencing God's wrath, thus saving us from God, and he will punish to the extreme any who refuse to believe this. God proves this by blessing us with wealth and prosperity, and as Fundamentalism-Evangelicalism play such a large role in the American middle class and amongst celebrities, it is little wonder everyone wants to jump on the glory bandwagon. It is good to have God on one's side after all.

Yes, I will challenge the theological pillars of this distorted "bad news," for bad news it is. It is not good news! It is horrible news. It is the same news that we have been hearing from long before Christianity came on the scene, long before Judaism came on the scene and long before that. It is the terrible story of two-faced gods. Sometimes they care for you, other times they seek to destroy you. The old gods are finally seeing their twilight as we begin the twenty-first century. Yes, it has taken that long since the gospel was first announced to have this kind of deep structural impact on our thinking and cultures—two thousand years of a long, slow, historical process of weaning from the fault that ensnares us all. But it is happening, and slowly but surely the authentic message of the gospel is beginning to reach the masses.

Those who have grown tired of simplistic answers to difficult questions will be richly rewarded as they begin to remove sacrificial thinking from their theology. This too takes time, but there is in the gospel a path to do this. In the last chapter we will take a cursory look at this path that changes our thinking for it involves the whole person. It goes by various names, but we will use the term "discipleship" when we discuss it. The follow-up book to this one will be titled *Liberating the Teaching of Jesus: Christian Discipleship in an Age of Crisis*. In this book we will break down the role that the gospel plays in helping us discard our sacrificial thinking. We will examine the practice and spirituality of Christian discipleship or following Jesus. Both books are practical in nature; this one focuses on our thinking, the next one on our action. When Jesus appeared on the scene his was a call to repentance, according to the gospel tradition: "Repent for the kingdom of God is at hand." Sadly, this has been misused, first by Catholicism, which wrongly grounded an entire penitential system on Jerome's Latin Vulgate translation, "Do penance." The Orthodox Protestant tradition would interpret this as a cry for a proper morality (always the social codes they lived by). To repent meant to follow the church's rules whatsoever they might be, usually reflecting a morality centered on sex and all of the bad things sex can lead to.

This is not gospel repentance. Gospel repentance causes us to realize that we have misread the Bible and misrepresented God. Gospel repentance is first theological repentance for we live our theologies. We act out what we think or believe. And of course, we justify how we act by citing our theology as its foundation.

Theological repentance involves the whole self. It means accepting that growth in the gospel is a continual shedding of our false views, paradigms or theories about who God is and how God acts. Once we learn to see the gospel through the lens given us in Jesus and certain parts of the apostolic tradition, it is impossible to go back to the sterile, soul-stealing propositions about God that have been foisted upon us in the name of a perfect God who wrote a perfect book. This beautiful, liberating message, that we are able to know and practice God's will, finds expression in Paul's letter to the Roman house churches. After challenging the opponents who were coming to Rome and disputing his apostolic authority, Paul ends up claiming that God does not discriminate against anyone, and in fact, God's mercy is so large as to include everyone, even our enemies. This causes him to break into a song of praise for this wonderful mystery that has been revealed. Then he says:

> I appeal to you therefore, brothers and sisters, by the mercies of God, to present your bodies as a living sacrifice, holy and acceptable to God, which is your spiritual worship. Do not be conformed to this world, but be transformed by the renewing of your minds, so that you may discern what is the will of God—what is good and acceptable and perfect. (Rom 12:1–2 ESV)

Let us look at what theological repentance looks like.

Theological repentance begins because of mercy, the kind of mercy God has shown us by coming into our world and showing us what love looks like. We are invited to the same kind of life Jesus lived, as one who freely offered his life in order to show us what the will of the Father was. This self-sacrifice on the part of Jesus (which we have not yet defined) was for him, and for us, a form of spiritual service. That is to say that self-giving is the mode by which God chooses to be known. Our lives become a sort of liturgy, a form of worship. How is this accomplished?

It involves two parts. The first has to do with no longer conforming to that which we see and know in and from our world, our culture. The second part is the flip side of the coin. As we learn how the world thinks and acts and how we have been raised to participate in this through parenting, school and church, through the gospel we also learn how to make the shift away from certain types of thinking and being-in-relation that do not work.

## Religion

This process is not an altogether easy one, as you know. It involves a true metamorphosis, a change in the way we think and act. It is sheer folly to think we are exchanging our set of cultural rules and norms for a religious one. If the world dances, drinks, and smokes, Christians do not dance, drink, or smoke. Religious rules like this have been around since the beginning. Further, we all know people who follow all of the rules of their church tradition who are miserable, petulant, proud, and self-righteous. Sure, Christians who follow the rules may look different from the bums, homeless, drug addled, and poor, but inside they look identical to the culture around them. They can't see this, but one wonders why these Fundamentalist-Evangelical Christians keep piling on the rules in the quest for purity or holiness which is never achieved.

Let me give you a silly example of this which could be multiplied exponentially. When I lived in Lancaster, Pennsylvania, there were many different types of Mennonites and Amish (Anabaptist) groups. How did one tell them apart? Some looked and dressed and behaved just like every other Jane and Joe. These were the liberal Mennonites. Conservative Mennonites looked different, or at least their women did. While the men dressed like other men of Lancaster County, the women wore long dresses and head coverings. Some Mennonites felt that having chrome on a car was worldly, it was too flashy, and so they would spray-paint the chrome black (and they always bought black cars). This was supposedly a car that would not stand out (no joke, they actually believe that, but boy does one notice them).

In the Amish community there were many different Amish. Some Amish can drive and use the local electrical grid and drive cars. This was too worldly for some Amish bishops who created rules that their members could not own cell phones, use electricity supplied by the power companies, and further they could not drive cars, but they could use horses and a buggy to get around. Even the buggies had to be different. Mennonites had all black buggies, Amish a mixture of black with grey side panels. Some Amish women used buttons on their dresses, but this was seen as a capitulation to worldly clothing, so others began to use just hooks. Others thought hooks were too worldly, so the women held their clothing together with straight pins. I kid you not.

Each group sought to outdo the other in terms of showing how holy they were.

Baptists are world renowned for their rules. Each Baptist group agrees on certain rules while others have their own specific rules for behaviors that they deem worldly and unacceptable. In small towns across America, Baptist churches compete for who can be the holiest, purest examples of what a godly life looks like. But the thing is that these Fundamentalist-Evangelical Baptists are just the same inside as the world they claim to reject. There is a certain irony in the fact that when you take a map of the United States and overlay Pornhub.com searches over it, the area of the country that lights up like a beacon is the Bible Belt. Take the same map and overlay it with teenage pregnancies and again the Bible Belt lights up. The Deep South in the US is obsessed with sex and sexuality, have all manner of ministries devoted to sexual purity (anyone remember the Bill Gothard seminars or purity rings?), yet can't seem to control the raging hormones that run through them. The same thing occurs if you lay a map of obesity on the US. Yep, it's the Deep South and all their potlucks. You can add rules to regulations, and laws to laws, but these do not change what is going on inside people.

To no longer conform to the world and to undergo a process of transformation does not begin in our behavior but in our thinking. We experience a transformation of our thinking first. Once that happens our behavior models that of Jesus, who was self-giving. In other words, God doesn't care if you dance, drink, eat, sleep, smoke, drive a car, or use a cellphone. We are fools if we think this is true. Our human rules are means by which we have a metric to judge others. We can look at one another's lives, and seeing which rules you obey or not, I can determine if you are the kind of Christian I can fellowship with.

Repentance in this religious way of thinking is always about morality. Christian repentance has to do with changing our minds about things, changing the way we understand and see life and people, transforming the thought patterns and processes that we inherit from our upbringing and education. But when Jesus urges repentance, it is always in the direction of self-giving, not morality. You don't find Jesus sounding at all like a holiness preacher, and there were plenty of them in his time. He could have done what they did and called Israel to repentance by obeying all of the laws found in Torah (Genesis through Deuteronomy, the books supposed to have been written by Moses). His contemporaries the Pharisees did such because they believed that if the people would obey the Torah God would bless the land. The Essenes taught the same thing, only they went even further in their quest for holiness. Yet time and again, Jesus appears to (and does) break with the legal interpretation of his contemporaries, coming into conflict with them over even the most basic of laws, the Sabbath laws. It is as if there is something far more important to Jesus than just getting people to follow the laws, and that more important thing is theological repentance. "Repent for the way God reigns is right here, right now."

It is the presence of this new way of understanding how it is that God reigns, how it is that God rules over all things, that occasions our ability to rethink what we thought we knew about God in the first place. Jesus's teaching, especially his parables, are suffused with the difference between how people perceived, understood, and talked about God and how he himself would understand and speak about God. Theological repentance is changing the way we perceive, understand, and think about God and the new way is given to us in the gospel.

A summary version might look something like this: We were made to imitate our Abba. However, we all take part in the system of wrong imitation of the "other," i.e., Adam imitating Eve. This imitation produces every form of violence (greed, gluttony, envy, etc.) as we all reach, grope, and grab to imitate others. We act like orphans, forgetting our loving Abba. In this imitation we try to differentiate ourselves from all "others" but end up imitating that which we wanted to be different from. We all imitate those around us not realizing it's the very thing that kills us, secludes us, and ostracizes us. In our search for uniqueness, individualism, and enlightenment of ourselves, we inherently become just like those around us, i.e., the fashion industry, high school clicks, businesses, etc.

However, Jesus came and showed us another way. The true way. The Way! He showed us the one true, life-giving path, found not in grasping as orphans, but in receiving an inheritance (true life and humanness) as children doing Abba's will (imitating Abba). Life is found in relinquishing to choose power to discriminate, exclude, and determine right and wrong (i.e., to judge, which is to eat of the fruit of the knowledge of good and evil). Instead, we give up that power and find true power in giving, pouring out, and emptying (*kenosis*) ourselves for the "other" like our Abba revealed himself in Jesus on the cross. This is the theology of the Cross. It is found in the true imitation of Abba laying down his life in sacrifice for all. This is the power of love (self-sacrificial, unselfish, and all for the "other"). It is this Way that Jesus came to show us, to model and live out. We are now called to take part in his life, walk his walk, and live imitating our loving Abba.

As I conclude this introductory chapter, I hope you can see some of the territory we are going to traverse and through which we shall express theological repentance. We will look at the classic doctrines of God, the Trinity, the humanity and deity of Jesus, his atoning death and resurrection, as well the Holy Spirit, the church, and most of all the Bible. Each doctrine will be subjected to repentance. In repenting we do not toss out these precious formulations nor demean their significance. To the contrary, we find that when understood through the lens of the gospel these doctrines become life-giving and make sense. As it stands, the way these doctrines are taught in American Protestant Christianity is, to put it simply, bullshit. Words and formulations are parroted with no understanding. There are often massive disconnects between doctrines. Some ways of understanding these doctrines border on the superstitious and it is little wonder the average churchgoer chooses to leave "theology" to the few.

Our need for re-interpretation is due to the barnacle tradition encrusted nature of these doctrines. They have been distorted and twisted all out of proportion. Doctrinal taffy, I suppose, is what to call it. Our desire for re-interpretation of these doctrines stems from our unwillingness to throw the baby out with the bath water as liberal Protestants have done. If Protestant Christianity in America is to survive it will need a foundation that is stable. This stability is provided by the tradition itself in the form of the baptismal creed of the early church, "in the name of the Father, the Son, and the Holy Spirit." The early Roman baptismal formula is what would be used to frame the so-called Apostle's Creed and later the Nicene Creed. I am not seeking to re-invent the theological wheel (again), nor am I claiming some sort of mystical divine revelation that bypasses the church tradition. What I am doing is showing you how to take the insights of the gospel and apply them to these great formulations, thus allowing the transformative thinking of the gospel to change you from a doctrinal caterpillar to a beautiful theological butterfly.

# 2

# Revelation

The best place to begin anything is at the beginning, and in our beginning is darkness. All we know is what we are told. We were the blind leading the blind. It is into our intellectual and spiritual darkness that a light shone, and this light comes from God and is God. Light illumines; it allows us to see what is all around us, and it also opens the way for us to see what is inside us.

There are two aspects of our darkness. The first is the role of deception, particularly self-deception. The second has to do with death, specifically the human fear of death and of what comes after death. We cannot understand our darkness, or even know that we are in darkness, until the Light shines and shows us how we have been deceived. We would not even be aware that we exist in darkness unless the light shone. Like fish in water, we live in the darkness of the mind and of the worldviews we have created to explain human history, good and evil, and the presence or absence of the divine.

There are plenty of biblical texts that testify to the darkness of our thinking, and the problem is our thinking. In our blindness we are like the six men who touch differing parts of the elephant, but we do not have any idea what others are sensing. The way we construct our reality is by plying together ideas and constructs that simply do not fit together, but the false sense of security we gain from trying to make them fit makes us think we are actually seeing something when we are not seeing anything at all.

The Christian tradition in the West has, since the early fifth century, called this the doctrine of original sin. The problem here is that "sin" was understood primarily in legal terms, as a moral failure, and thus God was conceived of as a Lawgiver and as Judge, Jury, and Executioner. It is true that sin is a moral failure, but it is far greater than that. There is a flaw in the human species, a fault as it were, that can take even the best of intentions and bring about bad circumstances. Even our best is flawed.

To say that we exist in sin is to say that we are born into a world and the way that world thinks and orders itself and its thinking. Sin is not just those things we do that are bad or our failure to do good when we ought to. Rather, sin is a power that structures all of our thinking, and thus the way we perceive reality.

The greatest sin of all, however, is to begin theology with the problem of sin. If we begin here, we will always fail to understand why it is that we do not seem to change. This is so because the solutions to sin we come up with theologically are false, because the problem that we created is false. If sin is just about morality, the solution is more law. This is a significant reason that so many have left the church; it is mired in sin management and functions as The Morality Police. It has misdiagnosed the problem and so the solution offered can only be a religious one, not one given in the revelation of the gospel.

The Christian tradition has always insisted on the priority of God revealing God's self, but rarely is this actually put into practice. Why? Because we confuse God's revelation with our religion, and we assume that the religious constructs we create are in alignment with God's revelation when they are not.

In a nutshell, and this will be something we see repeatedly in our little book, there is a massive difference, an infinite difference, between the way humanity has developed its views of the divine and that of the gospel revelation. There is a commonality to be found in all of the ancient views of that which is called "god" or the "gods." All the ancient gods are double sided, that is, the concept of divinity has aspects of both good and evil. It is easy to find example after example of this in just about any mythology. Outside of the Bible this arbitrariness between divinity as blessing and divinity as curse is managed by rituals, most notably sacrificial rituals. When we perceive the gods are not on our side, we offer up young men or women to volcanoes, or drowning, or ritual butchering. Somehow, or so our logic goes, the shedding of blood seems to appease the wrath or apathy of the god/gods so they will in turn bring us peace and prosperity. This is religion. Religion requires blood. It is true that we also find this kind of god concept in the Bible, but it is a concept that is slowly moving away from sacrifice. This is perhaps the most important contribution the Bible makes to our understanding of theology. We shall have much more to say about this in the next chapter.

The ancient gods were like vampires; from time to time they needed blood to satisfy their eternal hunger. You can read all about the history of ancient religion and its sacrificial practices in hundreds if not thousands of books produced in this past century as the discipline of anthropology (the study of what the human is and does) has developed. Here is the fact: we humans did theology first, before divine revelation. We constructed the category of the "god" prior to revelation. This means that revelation comes into religion and its first task is to disabuse us of our dualistic gods, sometimes favorable, sometimes terrifying.

The God revealed in the gospel is first of all Light (1 John 1:5). The God of the gospel is not a mixture of light and darkness, good and evil, Jesus and the satan. The God of the gospel has no dark side, no "shadow of turning." This means that our old view of divinity as arbitrary or capricious or apathetic or condemning is challenged. This is a huge hurdle for many because they have only ever known "God" to be such a character. Yet this is not what we see in the "Father of Lights from whom every good gift comes." Sadly, the Fundamentalist-Evangelical god has far more in common with the old gods, the gods of religion, than it does with the Father of Light. If your god looks more like satan than Jesus, you have got a serious problem on your hands.

If we begin with the axiom (the foundational statement) that God is light and in God there is no dark side at all, it is also possible to say that this light has a very specific character, which is love. In the New Testament this is *agape*, self-giving love for the other (1 John 4:8). The revealed God in Jesus Christ is not just Light and not just illumination, but Light as Love or Love as Light; love is an action but so is light. Light reveals and love heals. *This* is the God of the gospel.

Now I don't have a god concept. I don't need one because I know the one who has come into my world and has shown me the way and healed my psycho-spiritual brokenness. As Light and Love, the action of the one we call "Father" is always going to be oriented to that which is for our benefit. From this point on when I use the word "God" it is almost always with reference to the dualistic god concepts we humans created in our sick theologies; when I mention "the Father" it is always with reference to the divinity whom Jesus knew and trusted.

What the gospel seeks to help us understand is that the character of God is revealed in the actions of Jesus; it is therefore essential to note the way Jesus behaves with different groups of people. With the regular people, the majority poor and marginalized, Jesus announces the good news that the Father is also their Father, even if their culture says such is not the case. The broken hearted, those with a bankrupt spirituality, those who grieve about their life and the condition of their life, those who seek peace and pursue it, these are the ones who are blessed. Conversely, toward those who would on moral and legal-theological grounds classify these same underclasses as sinners, common folk, *am ha-eretz* (people of the land, "the deplorables"), Jesus has little sympathy. He finds them to be hypocrites, burden givers and liars.

You see, the Father is not in the business of discriminating between good and evil persons. At least according to Jesus, his Father makes rain to fall on the just and unjust and the sun to shine on good and evil. According to Paul, the Father sees this fault line that runs through all of us, and has judged us all as broken, so he is just to also forgive each of us and all of us (Rom 11). When the church preaches that God is in the business of judging what they really mean is that they are in the business of judging; to disobey the church, the priest, or the pastor is to disobey God.

This is all just fear-based religion; the revelation of the Father casts out all fear, for fear has to do with us, not with God.

Our task then is to distinguish revelation from religion while at the same time recognizing that revelation comes into the heart, the center, the very sacred of religion. In other words, while we can distinguish between the two, we cannot really understand one without the other. Think of it this way. Suppose you are a totally benevolent Creator, and yet humanity has already created a false view of what a god is. How do you come to the human species as a totally loving, peacemaking, merciful God of all when the humans have already decided that gods are both/and: light and dark, good and evil, loving and angry, merciful and judging? How do you do this? Well, first it would take time and great patience, and this is what we see in the Jewish tradition. It was to the Jewish people that Ha-Shem (The Name that cannot be spoken or YHWH) came and began a long historical process of weaning them from their sacrificial cultural background. This revelatory process culminated with the sending of the Son to live the life we know as Jesus of Nazareth.

What is sad is that this educational process moving us away from sacrifice has been subverted in Fundamentalism-Evangelicalism. The orthodox Protestant tradition has reverted back to the earliest part of the educational process of the Jews; they still see the divine in sacrificial terms. This is why for them, God (that is, their god concept) is a series of nouns and adjectives, all called attributes, which when put together do little more than create a Frankenstein-looking deity with religious and theological ideas from here, there, and everywhere, usually dead ones.

What we want to recognize is that there is not only an educational process of the Jews. After Jesus, this educational process continues as both Judaism and then Christianity, which began their two thousand-year walk together with the revelation of the Son. Have we learned anything in two thousand years? The answer is both Yes and No. Sometimes the light of the gospel shines through the Christian religion while at other times theologians, popes, pastors, councils, TV, radio, and internet hucksters and others muck it up, placing that light under the bushel of sacrifice.

What is said about God in the gospel? What is it that makes the gospel good news? If God is revealed as Light and not darkness, how shall we understand all those passages in the Bible where God is a Lawgiver, a Judge, sometimes even a murderer? How do we deal with the fact that "the Bible says" that God is angry, vindictive, etc.?

We are not the first ones to ask this question. It is quite old. There was a heretic in the second century named Marcion who had a bit of a disastrous understanding of this question, and when the problem of the "angry god" is brought up today, some Christians are quick to accuse those who ask it of heresy. And it is true that we also find the later Jewish rabbis dealing with this question rather vigorously at times. One of the purposes of allegorical interpretation (where the literal reading is rejected, and a symbolic interpretation is given) was to have a method that would understand those texts in a way that would put those concerns to rest.

If, for two thousand years Christianity has had this view of God, it is also true that this view of God has been challenged time and again, not only in Christianity but in Judaism as well. It has taken this long because the deception of religion is so strong. Worse, we have been told that if we question this view of God we will burn forever because we dared to challenge the holiness and supremacy of God. No. This is not the God of the gospel, nor is it the One whom Jesus called "Papa."

In one sense there is not a "doctrine of God" in the Bible. When people insist we take all references to "God" in the Bible and put them all together what we end up with is a two-faced deity, which I call a Janus-faced god. When we re-read the Bible in the light of the Jesus story, what we find is the key to unraveling all of the contradictory statements in the Bible about divinity. In the next chapter we will explore this key (and it is not a secret, it is quite visible in the text), but for now we want to learn to distinguish when the Bible is promoting the god of religion and where the revelation of the Creator, the Living God, is breaking through. It isn't rocket science but it does require a change in thinking because it is a paradigm shift. And once you see it you can't unsee it.

The fundamental problem seeks to understand why "God" is sometimes angry, sometimes sad, sometimes blessing, sometimes cursing, sometimes mercilessly judgmental, and other times mercifully kind. This brings us to the fundamental question of the relationship between the two Testaments and of the relationship of Judaism to Christianity. Is the New Testament an extension of the Jewish Scriptures? Or is it a contradiction of those same Scriptures? Is there a way that a path can be traced from antiquity to the present that allows us to see the effects of the gospel, and if so, how do we discern this?

Is the Bible mono-vocal, does it only speak with one voice, or are there multiple perspectives in the Bible between which we are invited to discriminate? If there are multiple voices, what is the discriminator? In Fundamentalism-Evangelicalism we were told that the whole Bible was God's voice, and yet the reason we are all where we are is because this theology just does not work in real life. It leaves us despairing when life gets tough, it leaves us hopeless when life gets overwhelming. We have found ourselves adrift in a sea of confusion with this God. Little wonder, for this two-faced deity would one day bless us and the next day curse us. This God was impossible to please even if we could figure out how to please him, which usually involved learning to follow a mish-mash of laws, or do's and don'ts.

It might be objected that Christians for thousands of years turned to this God in real faith and hope. And that is true, they did. But as one reads their testimonies what we always see them clinging to is the mercy of God. No one ever said they were glad God was strict and stern. No one ever rejoiced when they thought God was pissed at them. The Christians, who for the last two thousand years have believed in a Janus-faced God did so in fear and trepidation, even as the gospel explicitly says that "perfect love casts out fear."

Before we delve into the distinction between religion and revelation in the Bible, we want to note that the approach we are taking is very Jewish. I am contending that the Bible is a great debate, a debate between the false view of religion and the truth of revelation. This is a very Jewish approach to the Bible. After the destruction of the Temple in 70 CE, Judaism underwent a reconstruction. A century before the Christians began to close their canon, the Jewish rabbis had already produced their book to interpret the Jewish Scriptures (the "Old Testament"). It is called the Mishnah. Rabbi Judah the Patriarch composed the Mishnah around 200 CE. Now the remarkable thing about the Mishnah is that while it is slanted to the position of a certain way of thinking, it is inclusive of the debates around all manner of issues. Many times, you will read that Rabbi X says this, while Rabbi Y says that, and Rabbi Z says yet another thing. The Mishnah is not intended to make up your mind. It seeks to engage you, the reader in the debates and to cause you to ponder the mysteries of God and his Torah.

In the same way, in the next chapter I will show you this great debate in the Bible and how Jesus and Paul and others carried on that debate. But before we do that, we need to ask about that which allows us to discriminate between religion and revelation. Then we will be in a position to ask about the God who is revealed in the gospel.

Our starting point will be that of the apostle Paul who proclaimed the Good News as "Jesus Christ crucified." The event of the death of Jesus is that which allows us to see who God is and how God behaves towards us. Another way to say this is to say that God is in God's self the way God acts towards us. God's being is revealed in God's acts. We are not talking so much about atonement theory here (we will do so in a later chapter). What we want to understand is just how the story of Jesus's passion reveals the character of God.

Let me begin by asking you this question: in all the artistic representations and paintings of the crucifixion, how many times does one "see" God (the Father) in them? I'm not talking about modern sentimentalist art but classic art. The answer is none. Crucifixion paintings are morbid, sometimes grotesquely realist, always haunting and occasionally mind blowing. But one does not "see" God at Calvary.

Take a look at all four passion stories in the Gospels. The passion narrative technically begins with the arrest of Jesus in the garden and ends with his burial in the tomb. When you read this story, you will notice that God never makes an appearance. There is no divine voice proclaiming that Jesus should be listened to, there is no mighty warrior that comes down to save Jesus, there is no powerful God exerting power over those who would dare accuse, try, convict and crucify the Beloved Son. In other words, "God" does not save Jesus. Why? Where is God in the passion narrative?

One of the most beautifully artistic representations of God's presence at Calvary comes in the Mel Gibson-directed film, *The Passion of the Christ*.[1] As Jesus takes his final breath the camera angle switches to an eagle eye view, but this view is seen through a drop of water as it falls. This is not just rain; this drop is a teardrop and as it falls onto the dead Jesus we too are drawn into the sorrow of that tear. This is the only way possible to capture where "God" was that day. The Father was grieving.

Paul must have understood the death of Jesus this way for he tells the Corinthians (2 Cor 5) that God (the Father) was in Christ reconciling the world to God's self. Furthermore, he shares just how that reconciliation occurred. Paul noted that when it came to Calvary, God was no accountant. God had not kept a record of our rights and wrongs. There was no divine ledger where every little peccadillo, error, mistake, or intentional pain you caused others was kept. Where would Paul even begin to figure this out from?

One could perhaps point to Jesus's words from the cross, "Father, forgive them for what they do" (Luke 23), which also appear as Stephen is dying in the book of Acts (Acts 8). There are problems with this saying textually, meaning it is not found in certain manuscript families, and it has been claimed it is an editorial comment by the author of Luke-Acts. My own study has led me to feel comfortable tracing it back to the historical Jesus because it is totally congruent with his life and teaching. It is also possible this is an editorial saying, which just tells me that the author thought that what he was writing was congruent with Jesus's life and teaching.

I have to think that it was something like this saying that Paul may have been influenced by as he speaks of God's reconciliation in his letters. Apart from that saying it is difficult to take the other sayings from the cross and deduce what God was doing, if God was doing anything. The saying

---

1. Los Angeles: New Market Films, 2004.

then is our window into just exactly what was happening as humans murdered the Son of the Father.

It is Jesus's willingness to be killed and it was Jesus's desire to forgive that becomes his prayer, "Father, forgive them." I have two quick remarks. First, it is obvious that the Father heard the prayer of Jesus because there was no divine retribution. Second, if we understand the Father and the Son to share the same mission, the same values and the same mind, then Jesus knew his Father would indeed hear his prayer and forgive us this heinous act (and all other acts).

Jesus, in forgiving others as he dies, is doing something remarkable. He, unlike so many of the psalmists, does not cry out for vengeance or retaliation. His is a voice of a different order, a different reality. His dying voice reveals something far deeper and more profound than we can think or imagine (we shall look at this in a later chapter). Furthermore, his resurrection from the dead does not bring retaliation but peace, shalom, wholeness. His coming to all the different resurrection witnesses in peace would have absolutely forced them to reconsider the character of God, for they expected wrath and divine "justice."

The cross then is the nerve center of all our theology. What makes the crucifixion of Jesus different than the other tens of thousands crucified in the Roman Empire? The answer can be found when we compare Jesus's voice with other voices that speak to being killed by others. We have already noted many of the psalmists seek vengeance or justice from God, or some sort of divine retaliation. The first human victim, Abel, had a voice too. His voice sought vengeance or justice.

When you look at the most ancient compositions about the origin of creation and human society, commonly called myths, one tends to find that the voice of the victim is altogether removed or muted. In other words, the stories that myths tell of their social/group murder blames the problem on the victim, not on us, and the myth hides the murder while emphasizing the victim's guilt. In these myths the "victim" usually agrees with the community about the evil they supposedly did.

The Bible opens up this deception in mythology and the first victim, Abel, is recognized as "innocent." That is, he did not deserve what came to him (death). However, his voice is not the voice of the Father for Abel's voice, like so many of the psalmists, is a voice seeking retribution or vengeance. The writer to the Hebrews saw this when he said, "Jesus' voice speaks a better word than that of Abel." In other words, in the Bible we should expect to find all three voices, and we do: the voice of the victim of myths which is not heard, the retributive but random/innocent victim's voice and the voice of the forgiving victim on Calvary. It is only the last voice which is the voice of the Father.

This voice, this generously forgiving voice, reflects the character of the Father. Like the early church, we can say that where we see the Son we see the Father, and where we see the Father, we see the Son. Their character cannot be separated, nor can their activity be divided. They are one; the only distinguishing mark are the appellates (names) Father and Son.

This is the viewpoint most profoundly explored by the writer of the Fourth Gospel, commonly known as the Gospel of John. In the Fourth Gospel, the writer repeatedly makes clear that to speak of the Son is to speak of the Father and to know the Son is to know the Father. There is no separation between them. You could not drop a nanoparticle between them. They share the same "identity" ("being") and "character" ("actions").

Up to this point I have not said anything about the Holy Spirit and the cross. I have written more detailed observations elsewhere in my books on this, but for now let us again turn to the Fourth Gospel and the first letter of John to see that indeed the Holy Spirit is connected to the cross. He writes in his letter:

> Jesus Christ is the one who came by water and blood, not by water only, but by the water and the blood. And the Spirit is the one who testifies, because the Spirit is truth. For there are three that testify, the Spirit, the water and the blood and these three are in one accord. (1 John 5:6–8, my translation)

The writer in his Gospel does not seem to say much about the Holy Spirit except in John 7 and later in certain sections of the upper room discourse (John 13–17). These texts, when read in the light of the author's theological tendencies, all point to the double Holy Spirit–giving scene: the first comes when Jesus exhales his final breath on the cross (John 19). The true human "gives his spirit." The second is the upper room where Jesus breathes his Spirit upon the group of disciples and talks about forgiveness (John 20).

My takeaway from all this is that the way we speak of God, as Trinity, means that we do not view any aspect/mode/name of a figure in the Trinity as different from another. Whether we call upon God as Father, or see the Father in the Son, or the Spirit who bears witness to the Son, in each case we are not dealing with three different gods but three different ways of talking about the same divine presence. And it is the cross (and resurrection) that shows us this most clearly.

What is revealed in the death of Jesus is reconciliation. Or with the great Swiss theologian Karl Barth we can say that revelation is reconciliation. God reveals God's self not as a vengeful but as a forgiving deity, and before the death of Jesus, no god was ever known as such.

But we must deal with a complication with what we have been taught. Most of us learned to read all statements about God in the Jewish Scriptures as referring to the Father. This was certainly true of many in the early church. Even as they struggled to understand the intimate relation of the Father and the Son, which would culminate in the Nicene Creed of 325 CE, they also had to wrestle with how they appeared to be very different characters. As we noted before, the heretic Marcion raised this question. How could "God the Father" be so mean and vindictive while Jesus the Son appeared to be merciful and forgiving?

Let us briefly review a few important points. First, there are two perspectives within the Bible. These perspectives we have are called religion, which is sacrificial, and revelation, which is self-giving. The perspective of religion will always contain some element of violence. That violence can be muted or almost erased, but it leaves traces. The perspective of revelation, that God is Light and God is Love and furthermore, that God is One, is a perspective without sacrifice, without vengeance, without retribution and without violence or the need for blood.

Second, there are three voices in the Bible and the perspective of religion contains both the voice of the mythic guilty victim, and the voice of the innocent but vengeful/justice seeking victim. These two voices are both engaged in religion.

You might wonder why the Bible has three voices instead of one. Some might say that if God wrote the Bible false voices would not be included. Their view that God is perfect, God wrote the Bible, therefore the Bible is perfect is a nice syllogism, but it breaks down. Perfection in God is one thing, perfection in a set of human documents is another. If we put the two assumptions together, we would find ourselves in an endless attempt to try and harmonize everything in the Bible. We have seen just how convoluted that can become with over forty thousand types of Protestant churches all claiming they have "perfect doctrine." You know as well as I do, to disagree with their doctrine is tantamount to disagreeing with the Bible and ultimately disagreeing with God.

Why not recognize that indeed the Bible has multiple voices and that our task, under the guidance of the Holy Spirit, is to discern those voices? Now we do not do this willy-nilly, picking and choosing which verses or authors we like and rejecting the others. Rather, we use the revelation of God in Christ, reconciling the world to God's self in the crucifixion of Jesus as the key to the biblical cipher. This means that we do not understand Jesus's death as a sacrifice to appease an angry deity. It means we view the cross through the eyes of Paul and the writer of the Fourth Gospel, and therein see what is happening. When we see that the Gospel has the same structure as an ancient founding myth, we immediately see that we are dealing with a phenomenon we know all too well, which is testified to in the Bible over and over again: we see the attempt to blame Jesus for the current social woes. We see Jesus becoming a social scapegoat. We see the all-against-one mechanism.

We see the same drama playing out in the passion of Jesus that we read in the Joseph story in the book of Genesis. There, Joseph is perceived as a problem by his brothers who decide unanimously to get rid of him. Later, of course, after Joseph is elevated to a position of power, he is given the opportunity to deliver his brothers from a famine when they come to Egypt looking for a little welfare assistance. Joseph plays with them a bit, kidnapping his father Jacob's favorite son, Benjamin, and threatening to keep him. But Judah steps in to offer himself instead, and in that moment of self-giving Joseph reveals himself, breaks down, and all the brothers become one family again. This story of Joseph and the story of Jesus are different, but both are scapegoated, abandoned by all, and yet vindicated at the end of the story.

When the Fundamentalist-Evangelical tradition turns the Father of Jesus into a blood-seeking heavenly vampire it turns the gospel on its head. It fails to recognize that unlike all the other gods who need blood sacrifice, the Father of Jesus has no desire or need for any sacrifice at all (Heb 10). Sure, sacrifice is necessary for forgiveness "under the Law" but this same "Law" comes under intense criticism in certain apostolic writers, even the writer of Hebrews who says this. In the next chapter we will take this further, for now it suffices to show you that there is a movement, a trajectory in the Bible, that is completely missed in the Protestant churches. This move is the slow correction of our view as to what constitutes a god, and more so, what constitutes us as humans. Some early church fathers like Irenaeus and Clement of Alexandria took this approach to biblical and church history when they contended that the revelation of the Father as God was a slow historical educational process. Early biblical stories of God being angry are rewritten so as to remove violence further and further from God.

This kind of shaping of tradition occurs repeatedly in the Jewish Scriptures. So does the opposite, whereby an original text about a victim is turned into a story of the apathy and ego of divinity, for example in the book of Job. If we follow those scholars who say that the prologue to Job (chapters 1–2) and the epilogue of Job (chapters 38–42) were added later, what we have in chapters 3–37 is a sustained lament of a person who is being scapegoated. Here we see Job being coerced to just agree that he is the problem so that there will be unanimity. But Job refuses to do what mythical victims do and agree that he is the problem, unlike, for example, Oedipus in the Greek plays of Sophocles. The writer of the prologue and epilogue, like so many in the ancient world, just could not see that the violence against Job was human, so in line with early Second Temple Judaism, the writer creates a figure to blame, the satan. In other words, the writer to the prologue of Job has "re-mythed" the original discourse.

The servant of Isaiah in the Servant Songs (four of which are found in Isa 40–55), does not defend himself. In the Hebrew text it would appear that the writer is coming out of the fog of sacrificial thinking, but this is made clearer in the Greek translation of the text. The Septuagint translation is clear that God has nothing to do with the violence done against the servant, and even challenges that viewpoint of the Hebrew text!

In other words, the Bible is a long process of a written story that is often misunderstood by one writer only to be corrected by another. This self-correction is part of the pedagogical process of Judaism, and accounts for the early rabbis' willingness not to try and harmonize the Scriptures, but rather to enter into their debates. They, of course, were focused on the legal tradition, but the apostolic church took this one step further and began to apply this same critical orientation to the doctrine of God.

When the apostolic church began to understand the relationship of Jesus to "God" they did so in two ways. The first was to underscore that the life, teaching and ways of Jesus were also the ways of the Father. The second was as they perceived that the salvation wrought by Jesus was real, effective and this worldly while divine in origin. The question before us is whether the apostolic writers understood Jesus's death as a sacrifice to appease God, or if Jesus's death was something else, something far more profound and powerful than they could imagine.

It is essential that we see the solution as the first Christians did, so that we can diagnose the same problem they did. The problem was seeking to understand how it was that their expectations of a warrior Messiah fit with the story of the Jesus they knew, both crucified and resurrected. There is a most interesting story in Luke 24. On the road to the village Emmaus, the risen Jesus joins in with two other travelers and begins to ask questions about what was going on? The discussion turns of course to him, except like all the other resurrection witnesses, they do not recognize him. He is just a stranger.

Luke records that Jesus began to interpret the Jewish Scriptures to them. How nice, we think. Jesus did Bible study. Big deal. And, as Luke records, "he began with Moses and all of the prophets" and "interpreted to them the things written about himself in the Scriptures" (Luke 24:27, my translation). That's all well and good until we realize that the interpretive method Jesus was using and the interpretive method the Fundamentalist-Evangelical churches use are two totally different ways to view Scripture! If we read Luke carefully, indeed if we read the Gospels carefully, or even better, if we read the "historical" Jesus carefully, we will find a way of interpreting the Jewish Scriptures that is almost the opposite of what the Protestant churches teach as the way to read the Bible.

In the next chapter we will explore in some detail how Jesus, Paul, and the writer to the Fourth Gospel interpreted the Jewish Scriptures and much of what we find may astonish you. For now, we simply note that the Bible is in the process of re-traditioning. What I mean is this: first we have scribes correcting manuscripts, adding and deleting words and phrases that do not fit their theology. Second, we see translators changing the meaning of the text whether from Hebrew to Greek or Greek to Latin. Third, even within the Bible itself we see this process of re-interpretation. Deuteronomy famously re-interprets Exodus and Numbers, Chronicles reinterprets Samuel-Kings, the added prologue and epilogue to Job create a new interpretation. Second Isaiah re-interprets First Isaiah, 2 Peter reinterprets Jude, as Colossians uses Ephesians or Matthew reinterprets Mark and Luke reinterprets them both! Paul even reinterprets his own theology from the early letters to the Thessalonians in 41 CE and the later letters of 50–52 CE. The Bible is a great big fat re-interpretation of itself. It is constantly engaged in re-interpretation, whether for good or for ill, as it is passed on down through the ages.

The amazing thing about the Bible is its powerful message that has, in a very hidden and deep way, changed human culture. There have always been those who more or less saw a non-sacrificial version of Christianity. This has manifested in many different ways with mystics, scholastics, theologians, priests and popes, and lay orders. Even though the Bible is a mass of re-interpretation it has continually influenced world culture.

The Fundamentalist-Evangelical wants to distinguish God's word from human tradition and when they do so they think they are following in the footsteps of Jesus. They would be following more closely in his footsteps if they avoided the mistake of claiming that the Bible was the word of God while asserting that human tradition was anything anybody said that disagreed with them. Jesus does not do that.

First, there was no "Old Testament" in Jesus's day. Various groups held to various writings as having degrees of authority. Torah had the most. But even Torah could be superseded in some groups with other texts and community revelations. Some groups held that the Prophets had a secondary authority to Torah, others that they didn't. The "historical" books of the Jewish Scriptures had even less authority and even through the first century there were doubts about the authority of a number of books. There was no such thing as an Old Testament.

Second, when Jesus quoted the Scriptures, he did so quite selectively. He will often add words or phrases or omit words or phrases. I have shown this in my book *The Jesus Driven Life*. Jesus appears to use Scripture as a foil to justify his mission and message. Paul follows a similar pattern in that when Paul does cite the Jewish Scriptures he does so in a similar fashion to Jesus; Paul omits or adds words or phrases to the biblical text he is quoting. The Fourth Gospel goes so far as to distance Jesus from the authority of Torah, and in that book the "Law" is always "your law" not "our law."

Third, when some Jewish traditions would argue that Torah was divinely inspired, they would use the Wisdom passage of Prov 8 and go on to claim that all things were created through Torah and that Torah was the light of the world. Sound familiar? Sure it does. The Fourth Gospel sets in contradistinction Jesus, the Word of the Father made flesh, and Torah, given through a human intermediary, Moses. Paul will go so far as to remove that authority, even further claiming Torah was given by angels (Gal 3), and that is not a good thing.

We have many reasons not to start our thinking with the viewpoint that the Bible is divinely inspired. Rather, following Jesus and his Jewish tradition, we have many more reasons for reading the text critically. If we do so we have to immediately recognize that Jesus did not derive his doctrine of God from "studying the Bible." Jesus's Father is only sometimes similar to Israel's God, and this is because, as we have seen, the Father was slowly revealing his character over a long period of time to a people who really did not want to change.

The warning to us then is this: when the gospel comes to us, we are invited to see "God" differently. God is not Janus-faced or two-sided.

What kind of God is revealed in the gospel? Earlier I said that the Christian tradition in the second and third centuries began to use the common three-part baptismal formula of the Roman churches, "I baptize you in the name of the Father, the Son and the Holy Spirit." This would become known as the doctrine of the Trinity. This doctrine has confused many for millennia, partly because we have used poor definitions. For example, Tertullian, a Latin-speaking lawyer at the beginning of the third century, began to use the term "persona" to refer to each figure in the Trinity. This suggested that there were three Gods, each self-subsisting, each with their own will and mind, each existing independently from each other. This would degenerate over time into a dispensationalizing of God's work: there is the time of God (presumably the Father) in Israel's history, then comes the time of the Son, Jesus, and now we are in the time of the Spirit/church. Furthermore, various attributes of divinity would be attributed to the Father, others to the Son, and yet others to the Spirit. Over time, this philosophical speculating would enhance views of God in Christianity that all but beggar belief. The Father is pitted against the Son and the Holy Spirit is too weird to figure out. The doctrine of the Trinity became a "mystery" for most, unexplainable, unknowable, or bizarre. Such is the Western view of the doctrine of the Trinity that Muslims can rightly claim Christians do not believe in one God but three!

The good news is that there is a place for the doctrine of the Trinity, but it is not to be located as an object of belief. Rather, the Trinity is not something Christians believe in, but something they believe through. The doctrine of the Trinity replaces the doctrine of the theory of the inspiration of the Bible and gives us a healthy and beneficial starting point.

The Christian doctrine of the Trinity was not an afterthought in early Christianity. It was soon apparent, even to the early Jerusalem community, that Jesus had a special relationship to the God they now knew as their Father. Early Jewish Christian understanding of Jesus may not have been as developed as we find in Paul or the Fourth Gospel, but it is clear that these Christians knew that in the life and teaching of Jesus they had a crystal-clear revelation of the character of God. Admittedly, this group had a hard time trying to fit Jesus within a Second Temple sacrificial framework. On the other hand, we can see them working this out in literature ascribed to them like James, 1 Peter, or Matthew.

It is true that it is rare to use the term "God" for Jesus in the apostolic writings. "God" had become redefined as "Father": caring, loving, forgiving. It is also clear that Jesus's elevation to the right hand of the Father (so to speak) involved the recognition that the Father bestowed upon him the unmentionable name, "Ha-Shem" the name above all names, the name of the God above all gods (YHWH) (see Phil 2).

One cannot distinguish the Son from the Father. How the Son behaves is a pure reflection of how the Father behaves. It would take three hundred years for the church to figure out how this all played out in terms of Greek philosophy, and another fifty years to figure out how to talk about the Holy Spirit as "God." Eventually we would receive the Nicene-Constantinopolitan Creed of 381. It is a beautiful piece of theological work, but it is not the last word that can be said on the trinity.

The twentieth century saw a great revival of the doctrine of the Trinity, beginning in 1932 with the publication of Karl Barth's *Church Dogmatics*. An explosion of books on the Trinity came onto the market in the late 1950s and has not stopped. Great theologians like Jurgen Moltmann, Catherine LaCugna, Karl Rahner, Ted Peters, Thomas Torrance, and so many others contributed to a revival of trinitarian thinking. There is still so much to mine in this literature.

One of the things I take away from the modern discussion has to do with the concept of person. What do we mean when we say God is three persons in unity? What, exactly, is a person? It was the early third-century lawyer/theologian Tertullian who introduced the Latin word *persona* into the discussion. The Greek-speaking Eastern churches never adopted this term, instead preferring the (difficult to translate into English) term *hypostasis* or *energeia*.

It is not so important to ask about what the Latin-speaking church thought about *persona*, we can simply note all the attendant conundrums as it relates to understanding Jesus: if Jesus is both human and divine, does he have two wills, two minds? How do these all relate? These questions produced all manner of replies, many of which were deemed heretical. The better question is, "What does the average person understand by the term person and how does this relate to 'God' as three persons?"

The largely accepted working definition of a person is as an island, a being that makes social contracts with other beings wherein both perceive themselves as completely independent. A person is one who makes their own choices and is captain of their own destiny. All of their desires and thoughts come from within themselves.

If such is the case, then no wonder the doctrine of the Trinity makes no sense. How can there be three persons in God? Three minds, three wills, three centers of emotion? How do they relate? It has become fashionable to refer to "God as community" but this doesn't suffice, because it tells us nothing about the divine community and how it operates (and saying they all love each other is saying nothing at all).

But what if this working definition is no longer valid? What if the human and biological sciences show us something else about what constitutes "personhood"? What if our definition of ourselves has to change before we can begin to understand how to redefine our understanding of God? And what if the ability to redefine ourselves comes about because Jesus redefines the character of God for us?

The twentieth century saw a massive change in our self-understanding. In literature, psychology, anthropology, sociology, philosophy, and other early humanistic disciplines, the notion of the person as an isolated individual began to come under intense scrutiny. The human mind was conceived of as a "communal structure" (Freud, Jung), the art world began moving away from "realism" (Picasso), humans were studied as groups (Levi-Strauss), and in literature the move away from the "author" began. By the time we reached the twenty-first century the biological and environmental sciences were contributing to our understanding of ourselves as a rather complex set of relations.

If we take our cue from all of the sciences rather than trying to impose pre-modern definitions on the discussion a significant change occurs. We no longer understand who we are as individuals; rather, we know ourselves only as persons-in-relationships. In other words, the "I" that is my "conscious self" is not me, for I can only exist in terms of my relations to other persons or the creation (or to God). In other words, I am not an "individual" in relation to other "individuals" I am "interdividual." I am my relationships. Who I am, what I think, what I want or desire all can be found not inside me, but inside my relations to others. In our modern world this relationality reaches beyond just human connection; it is now human connection technologically. I have a relation to my computer, my phone, my tablet, my TV as much as I have a connection with my wife.

By recognizing this I can, for the first time, also realize that wanting what others deem valuable will not make me any happier than I am. I can let go of desiring what other people around me or my culture wants me to desire. Since my desires are not my own but are imitations of other's desires, by analyzing my desires I can find where I have been co-opted by "the world." But I can only do so if there is an infinite resource that can truly meet all of my true needs and desires, and not only mine but yours as well. In other words, there has to be a source of infinite desire fulfillment for all, so we are not caught up in trying to desire even this from another, but only from Jesus.

When we desire the Father as Jesus desired only the Father, we find ourselves contemplating all the time as we go through life, about how best to speak and love and forgive and support and nurture, even as we are so cared for by God, our Father. If, however, we seek to fulfill our desires by looking at our parents or neighbors or friends (or enemies), we will never be satisfied.

Suffice it to say that there is a lot of evidence that humans are socially constructed. That fleeting sense of consciousness we have of ourselves and the knowledge that there is far more to us than we think or know is common to just about everybody. We must shift our understanding away from perceiving ourselves as isolated "persons" and learn to view ourselves as "persons-in-development-in-community." Each relationship we have affects us for good or for ill.

If we are "persons-in-development-in-community" this is because we humans are locked into a pedagogical space-time reality. Such is not the case for "God." God is one, singular, unique, not consisting of three separate "selves." God is One Self, who in the process of revelation, reveals exactly God's self. That is, God's revelation and God are identical. We choose to follow the apostolic tradition and recognize Jesus of Nazareth as the Word of God, as the one who is "the express image of God," the "Son of the Father," the one in whom the Father dwells completely and fully. The Bible, as such, is not the Word of God.

Again, as we learn to differentiate the religious noise from the harmonious revelation in Scripture, we do so by looking through the lens of the Trinity. Anything we say about the Son has to also be said about the Father and the Holy Spirit and vice versa. We do not follow those who dole out certain attributes or functions to the Father, still others to the Son, and the last few kooky ones to the holy Spirit. We do not follow those who would divide up God's activity in terms of time or history, who "dispensationalize" God. There is no need since we do not begin with the same understanding of "person" as they do.

Our understanding of the character of God is not a denigration of the Jewish Scriptures. They are chock full of revelation. They also contain a fair amount of religion. The Christian Scriptures (the New Testament) are not immune from this. They also contain a lot of revelation, but as we might expect, we also find certain elements of the early church that do not get it, and so religion enters back into the mix (this is known as the issue of the "Law" in relation to the gospel).

We do not differentiate between the Two Testaments as though the Jewish Testament was religion, and the Christian Testament was revelation. That is one of the problems of the heresy of Marcion. Rather, we recognize that both streams, religion and revelation, the sacrificial and the non-sacrificial, truth and deception, gospel and law, run through both Testaments. It is our task to "rightly divide the Word of Truth." Let's go back to Marcion and show that what I'm proposing here is quite different from Marcion's solution.

Marcion recognized that the God which the Christians proclaimed had a different character than that ascribed to God of the Jewish scriptural tradition. Marcion also believed that a good portion of the apostolic church had managed to assimilate the gospel message to the meta-narrative of the judgmental god found throughout the Jewish Scriptures. Some may think that like Marcion we are engaging in a "rejection of the Old Testament." They could not be more wrong.

Marcion (circa 110–50) rightly perceived a huge chasm between the message of the apostle Paul and that of Jewish Christianity. Inasmuch as the theology of Jewish Christianity was embedded in the narrative of Second Temple Judaism, it also included eschatological and/or existential judgment often conceived of in terms of retribution, often labeled as divine justice (which went under the rubric *dikaiosune theou*). The argument was framed to focus on God's holiness and human sin. God was righteous to condemn sinners (usually gentiles, but also "apostate Jews" or the *am ha-eretz*), for they had strayed from the path of holiness or righteousness.

Marcion perceived Paul as announcing another message, the gospel of the gracious God who forgives all freely. Marcion's solution to this problem was not simply to "reject" the Jewish scriptures. Marcion contended that there were two gods; one a demiurge who created all things and who inspired the Jewish scriptures, and the other the God and Father of Jesus who inspired Paul.

Marcion, in other words, believed in "gods" plural. It is this henotheism that was rightly rejected by the second-century church fathers. Marcion, like so many second-century "heretics," posited a dualism between creation and redemption, between the created reality and "spiritual" reality. He believed that created reality, the world of the flesh, the world of the material, was evil. It was the work of God to deliver us from this evil material world and to rekindle the spark of divine life within the "redeemed" so that they could escape the vicissitudes of the created reality. A part of this thinking is of course Platonic; the real (the eternal and unchanging) could not be found in the temporal, changing reality of creation. Thus, salvation was the flight to the eternal.

Inasmuch as the god of Judaism was a second-tier god (and Marcion believed that God existed), that God had created all things, but that god could not be the spiritual God of Paul and Jesus. The god of Judaism, for Marcion, was just like all the other gods of humanity; vengeful and vindictive and not the superior God, the God above all, the Supreme god. What Marcion rejected then was first not the Jewish canonical tradition, but the God who was vengeful; only secondarily were these Scriptures to be dismissed because they testified to this god as the Supreme god.

Were there early church fathers that laid a foundation? And if they did, and if it was on sand, would we want to follow them in this? We might ask then whether the solution to Marcion's problem (the two-faced God), offered by apologists like Justin Martyr and Tertullian was really a solution. We *might* ask that, if we are not afraid to admit that they too may well have answered this question incorrectly. But that would mean we would be criticizing the patristic fathers, and many are loathe to do that.

I argued in *The Jesus Driven Life* (chapter 4) that Justin Martyr's solution to the problem framed by Marcion between the "two gods" was not the best answer, and one that has left Christianity suffering under the false illusion that God is retributive for two thousand years. Justin used the Jewish Scriptures, as a whole, to demonstrate that Jesus fulfilled prophecy whether those Scriptures were revelatory about the Father of Jesus, or about the revengeful, retributive deity. In other words, whereas Marcion sought to eliminate the dark side from divinity, the early church fathers brought that in through the back door of their theologies.

Some today want so badly to believe that they are faithfully representing the "orthodox" position of the second- and third-century apologists. They may well be, but because they simply assume that the patristic fathers were correct in their response to Marcion, they perpetuate the same problems as their alleged forebears. They end up seeking to bring together that which God had sundered in the life and teaching of Jesus of Nazareth, which Marcion (and Paul) correctly noted, viz., violence and the sacred. And so, they continue to contribute to the muddying of the gospel with the attendant sacrificial interpretation which is necessary to justify such a move.

Some, like Justin Martyr, are supersessionist. They must engage in some trickery in assigning attributes to this and that member of the Trinity. They must break God into dispensations, arguing that God acts one way in one period of time and another way in another period of time. All of these solutions proposed by Christian apologists are just as bad, if not worse than that proposed by Marcion, yet they cannot see this. They are blinded to the real questions raised by Jesus and Paul because they have an unconscious need to defend what they think is orthodoxy.

Some believe that they are faithful to the orthodox heritage of Christianity when they claim to affirm the Nicene Creed. What they do not see is that their affirmation of the Creed is really nothing more than a bait and switch: they claim to be trinitarian monotheists, but when one puts their doctrine of the Trinity under critical scrutiny, what one sees is in fact a form of Marcionism: the temporalizing of God. In this view only two ways of thinking are possible. Either one must find a way to speak about God changing, or they must make God look like all the other gods, Janus-faced. Of course, by the time we got to the sixteenth century this problem was "resolved" by the penal substitution theory of the atonement of John Calvin. And as much as I respect Calvin, I think he made a very critical error here that has haunted us ever since.

The desperate need to have a perfect Bible, a perfect revelation, has ever been the bane of Christianity. Many cannot see the gospel because they have been blinded by the god of this age—the god of sacred violence, the god of religion, the god of all human culture. This god is a god made in our own image. The work of René Girard has scientifically critiqued this Christian view of god in the most devastating manner. Unlike all Enlightenment critics who engaged in a form of Marcionism by dispensing with the Bible or relegating it to religious fantasy land, Girard insisted that the Bible brought something to the table, a revelation that could not stem from the default juxtaposition of violence, and the sacred found in all human religion.[2]

In summary, the failure of Marcion and the early church fathers is the same failure as that of Protestant orthodoxy: the failure to rightly divide the Word of Truth between religion and revelation. This division is crucial if we are to understand the revelation of God as Father, Son, and Spirit correctly. If we fail here, if we allow sacrificial thinking into the non-sacrificial gospel, then what was once truly Good News becomes the same old bad news of all the other gods, of all the other human religions we have constructed.

---

2. Hardin, *Reading the Bible with René Girard*.

# 3

# God and the Bible

One of the first things we learned when we entered the Protestant tradition was that "All Scripture is inspired by God" (2 Tim 3). From this verse an entire theory of biblical inspiration was born. We soon learned words like infallibility and inerrancy. We were taught to trust our Bibles, that they only spoke the truth, the whole truth, and nothing but the truth. In short, our Bibles became the revelation of God, so much so that we would refer to it as The Word.

We were soon engaged in Bible study, but it quickly became clear to almost all of us that the Bible was not only a big book, it was also a very confusing book. But we took the word of our pastors that what "they" were teaching was the Bible and the Bible alone. When the confusion persisted a lot of us chalked it up to our own ignorance. It seemed to us that this business of who God is and what God wanted changed over time, but we were taught to adhere fast to the "eternal" (which meant "moral") principles of the Bible. Depending on the particular kind of Protestantism we were acquainted with, these "eternal moral principles" could run from slightly loose to incredibly strict with a thousand variations in between. While we dared not admit it, Bible study became a chore to be dreaded rather than a fulfilling discipline.

The default position of inerrancy, or of the Bible as God's word, is a latecomer to the game. It is a doctrine that finds its first awakening in the 1600s and it will bud, blossom, and flower in the eighteenth and nineteenth centuries. It is not an essential Christian doctrine for a number of reasons.

First, early followers of Jesus did not put their trust in a book, they trusted the Risen Lord Jesus who was with them by the Spirit. That is, early Christianity was created out of trusting that the Father is who he says he is, as revealed on earth in Jesus and in our hearts by the Spirit. One and the same God. Trust is to be given to God and God alone.

Second, it is a totally reactive doctrine. It cannot, and will not, look at the evidence before its eyes. While it is true that contemporary Evangelical scholarship has gotten better and is at least able to converse with critical biblical scholarship, the same cannot be said for Fundamentalism which knuckles down hard on inerrancy. Most defenses of inerrancy border on the absurd in a never-ending attempt to redefine what an error is so as to be able to accommodate "alleged contradictions."

Third, the doctrine of inerrancy is not a doctrine derived from the Bible, but one created by Christian theologians in order to buttress the authority of their interpretation over against their critics. It is not a doctrine but a method of interpreting the Bible, one that is for the most part hidden from you. The problem of inerrancy is that it codifies a sacrificial interpretation that requires that God be Janus-faced.

Fourth, those who use 2 Tim 3:16 in order to justify trying to squeeze inerrancy out of this verse (in tandem with other verses) do so dishonestly. An honest reading of the text allows for the translation, "All Scripture is inspired by God and is useful for . . ." but it is also possible to justify the translation, "Every Scripture which is inspired by God is useful . . ." Furthermore, the doctrine of inerrancy is said to apply to the Hebrew text of the Jewish Scriptures when in fact, it is the Septuagint, the Greek translation of the Scriptures that is used by the writer. And even furthermore, in the previous verses which mention Jannes and Jambres, the writer is quoting from the Aramaic tradition of the Targums! So which Scripture is inspired, the Hebrew, the Greek, or the Aramaic? Do you see the problem here?

A theory of the inspiration of Scripture is not necessary in order to highly esteem the biblical canon(s). In fact, the inerrancy theory is a rather low theory of Scripture because it replaces trust in God with faith in a book. I mentioned in the last chapter that the Bible is a great big debate between sacrificial religion and non-sacrificial revelation. To recognize this debate is to do no different than other Jewish scholars and teachers of Jesus's day and after. To see the different behaviors of God was something the rabbis had to deal with. At first, they understood the term "Elohim" to refer to the favorable, beneficent "aspect" of God, while Ha-Shem (YHWH, the

Unpronounceable Name) referred to the judging and vengeful "aspect" of God, but they later flipped this around. The point is, even they were trying to figure out who this God was and how this God acted. We see this shot through the Jewish Scriptures as "God" is having to reveal something utterly different about what a "God" is and how a "God" is known. One of the beautiful things about reading the Jewish Scriptures is to see how time and again writers and editors are constantly dealing with this. It becomes very clear in the Septuagint, where passages that are clearly sacrificial in the Hebrew Scriptures are translated non-sacrificially in the Septuagint. Isaiah 53 is a great example and E. Robert Ekblad has a splendid essay on this in the book *Stricken by God?*[1]

The Bible is an invitation to a story: the story of a Creator of Love and Light who brings redemption to a creation oriented to hate and death. The dominant motif used to describe this darkness in which we dwell is "exile," that is, as a species we are not where we were meant to be. The Bible tells a great big story from beginning to end, but it tells the story in such a way that we are given multiple beginnings and multiple endings, depending on how deeply embedded any given writer or editor is in sacrificial thinking.

Jesus Christ crucified is the great break in human sacrificial thinking. He is the Light that penetrates our darkness. How is this so? It all begins with the cross of Christ. If we assume that the entire Bible is inspired, jot and tittle, we will ultimately end up reading the death of Jesus through a sacrificial lens. We will be forced to. But if we look at the Bible through the lens of the Trinity, it becomes possible for the death of Jesus to radically alter all of our concepts of God and things theological.

When I teach this, I begin by asking where is "God" (the Father) in the passion narratives? From the garden of Gethsemane to the burial in the tomb, God does not appear to be present. It appears Jesus dies alone. It is at this point that the sacrificial answer is often given, that God cannot be present because God made Jesus to be sin and God cannot look on sin. And further, God was pouring his wrath against sin out on Jesus. It would be possible to conclude this if God was Janus-faced. But neither premise is warranted from the text. They stem from certain views of God, sin, and death.

If we realize that Jesus consistently trusts his Father through the crucifixion, then even the citation of Ps 22 becomes clear. Jesus cites the opening lines of the psalm to bring to the minds of his hearers what they are doing:

---

1. Ekblad, "God Is Not to Blame."

they are using him as a scapegoat. It is the all-against-one mechanism that is being revealed. Even Caiaphas nods to this when he says, "It is better that one man die than that the nation perish" (John 11). The citation of Ps 22 gives voice to the experience of one who has been horribly, wrongly blamed by society and seeks vindication from God. In other words, a non-sacrificial rendering of this part of the passion narrative is just as valid, if not more valid than a sacrificial reading.

In many of my books and essays I have tackled many of the verses about Jesus's death and for a more in depth look you may wish to consult them. Here I will summarize a few important findings.

First, Jesus's death has the same structure as "myths of origin." This was first shown by René Girard and mimetic theory. Myths, according to this theory, are false, not so much as explanatory stories of phenomenon that humans cannot explain, but false in that they are deceptive: behind ancient myths lie traces of a real victim who was blamed by the community and sacrificed. The gospel is the anti-myth. It has the same structure. It unveils the all-against-one mechanism used during social crises, but instead of hiding the victim behind some alleged guilt, it instead exposes Jesus's persecutors for what they are: human beings who do not realize or understand that they are stuck in a system that they do not control, and who justify killing (in the name of religion or the state) the one deemed guilty of upsetting the tranquility of the community or society.

By taking on the same form as myth, the gospel is able to decode, or deconstruct, or reveal the problem with human mythology and the way we tell our stories about those we marginalize, ostracize or kill. Jesus's death reveals two very important things: It shows humans reconstituting themselves (their society) around a single victim, and second, it demonstrates the Love of God. What we do not have in the passion that we find in mythology is the "God who comes to save the day" (deus ex machina). There is no Superman god that swoops in to save Jesus from death. This alone ought to radically call into question the belief that God is an "interventionist" deity. It means something that there is no radical saving of Jesus by God. The Father lets the Son die, or even more, the Father allows us to murder his Son. Our human propensity to use a little violence to stop our fear of greater violence is on display on Calvary. So is our human tendency to cover it up: blame Jesus (as does one thief and others), blame God (as do those who advocate for Penal Substitutionary Atonement), blame the devil (not too many do this, but it has been done), blame anything but don't blame me! I didn't do it.

There is proof that there were already attempts to mythologize Jesus's death. In Matthew's Gospel we find a conspiracy theory that the disciples had stolen the body. Elsewhere later, there would be stories suggesting Jesus didn't actually die and was revived in the tomb, and there is a very silly theory that it was Jesus's brother James who was mistakenly crucified not Jesus. Each of these in their own way seek to remove any trace of human culpability when religious authorities and the Roman state carry out the execution of Jesus.

The reality of violence and the Gospel's structural similarity to myth might not be enough to convince us this is the problem. Enter the Pharisee Saul of Tarsus, who would carry on this program and approve the lynching (stoning) of the early Greek-speaking Jewish Christian Stephen (Acts 8). Notice that when Paul is addressed by Jesus he is not asked if he wishes "to be saved so he might go to heaven someday." He isn't asked if he has behaved well. Instead comes the piercing question that will hurtle young Saul down a life's path he could not have imagined. "Saul, Saul, why do you persecute me?"

This divine question of persecution is before all of us and it is this question alone that, like Paul, truly blinds us. Why do we need justice? Why do we think we need retribution or retaliation or an equaling of the balance? Like Saul, until we take this question in and ponder it, we will not know just what it is that was accomplished on Calvary. If we are honest however, we will find ourselves examining our own propensity to justify our anger and hostility. We will begin to see how we have been involved in groups that targeted another and blamed them for the group's crisis. Families do it, schools do it, institutions do it, governments do it, clubs do it, and churches, synagogues, and mosques do it. There is hardly a human group to be found that does not distinguish itself from "the other" nowadays, usually around race, gender, religious or political affiliation, or nationality. Everybody blames everybody else, but if everybody is to blame then no one is to blame! This is hardly realistic.

Not only does God not rescue Jesus, God does something remarkable. In the act of Jesus dying, there is an expression of divine grace: God hears the prayer of the Son not to prosecute those who are killing him. Jesus does not seek justice on the cross. This is crucial. Humans seek justice. Jesus sought mercy through forgiveness. What we call justice is not God's justice, it is simply the human (sinful) tendency to demand requital or some form of payment. Divine justice is mercy such as Paul saw (Rom 11). If God were "just" in the way we are "just" there would have been a reckoning at the cross. Instead, the apostle Paul notes that God had no ledger, no account of wrongdoing at the cross (2 Cor 5). Instead, God, by demonstrating such gracious, loving forgiveness, reconciled us to God's self. We were made one with God because God is not a bookkeeper. One might say that the Father is averse not so much to sin, as to keeping track of it! Sin is not the Father's problem. From the divine perspective, sin has been overcome by being dismissed. It doesn't count or is not accounted. Only a Janus-faced God or a satan insists on sin record-keeping and prosecution.

Second, Jesus's death was not a sacrifice required or demanded by the Father. This is the big lie of PSA and of any sacrificial reading. It makes the Father out to be a sick vampiric deity more hung-up on morality than love. Hebrews 10 and the use of Ps 40 within it make this abundantly clear. The exegesis of Ps 40 in Heb 10:8–10 is one of the most critical exegeses in the New Testament and yet to our detriment it is frequently overlooked. In the sense that the author of Hebrews discerns a crisis in the old sacrificial system, he exposes its weaknesses and limitations and transcends the old with the new. René Girard has done this as well, only he uses the language of ritual, myth, and prohibition.[2] That is, the violent underpinnings of religion that have previously been ignored are now shown to be false through the revelation of the all-against-one victimage hypothesis which occurs in the biblical writings.

Those texts that reveal the victimage mechanism and the relation of violence to the sacred are texts concerning that about which one can speak of revelatory significance. These texts have the power to deconstruct other texts and themselves. Perhaps in this sense one can speak of an inner biblical interpretive approach (or hermeneutic).

The author of Hebrews saw the distinction between revelation and religion when he contended that God neither wanted sacrifice nor was he pleased with it. Yet, the law required them. This is the conundrum that faces the exegete, who, if not prejudiced by theological assumptions, will have to admit that Marcion lurks at the door, yet with good cause.

Yet if the law required sacrifice but God neither wants nor is pleased with it, what does this say for the non-sacrificial critique of the law? Only this: just because a text claims God is speaking does not mean God is speaking. Rather, any notion of the word of God or God's revelation must come under the truly critical control of the distinction between religion, which

---

2. Girard, *Things Hidden from the Foundation of the World*.

grounds violence, and revelation, which is non-sacrificial. Sacrifice and violence have never been part of the divine economy; as one early Christian letter put it, "violence is no attribute of God."[3] Perhaps the opening hymn in Heb 1:1–4 is meant to initiate this critical approach when it speaks of ways and means in which revelation earlier took place. But now God speaks through his intermediary, the Son, Jesus.

One could point to the passion narrative as giving us a head's up of this in the conversation Jesus has with the other two insurrectionists crucified with him (remember Jesus was tried and found guilty of insurrection). The one sought a deus ex machina, a superhero interventionist God. He was rebuked by the other who noted their guilt but Jesus's innocence. We have here, side by side, two interpretations of God and the death of Jesus. The first is sacrificial and either would demonstrate that "God" was not on Jesus's side or that Jesus couldn't possibly be the big bad Messiah they were hoping for. It's opposite recognizes that Jesus is being scapegoated and seeks Jesus's aid in the afterlife. Jesus promises him vindication. We recall Caiaphas (John 11) who would use Jesus as a scapegoat to unite the national leadership, and hopefully the people as well.

Romans 3:23–26 is often cited as proof that Jesus's death was a sacrifice, a propitiation for our sins. It is questionable whether "propitiation" is the best translation, modern translators now understand the noun (*hilasterion*) to refer to the "place where reconciliation occurs." Paul is saying our reconciliation takes place in Jesus. Furthermore, as Bob Hamerton-Kelly pointed out, Jesus's death might be a propitiation, but we have inverted the actors. More so, Jesus's death does not take place in some dark hidden space but is done publicly. We are the ones who think that in sacrificing Jesus we are doing God's will, and furthermore, we think God is involved in this by requiring it. In reality the Father offers the Son to us. It is we humans who are angry, vindictive and retributive. It is we humans who require blood, for all religion requires blood. It is *we* who are "propitiated" by God.

The Father did not need the death of the Son in order to be reconciled to us. But because we did it, we killed Jesus, the Father used our most basic structuring impulse as a species, the blame game, to rescue us from it, by becoming part of it, so that from the inside out it could be revealed for what it is: human religion.

In short, the gospel is the undoing of all that which is evil in the world. It exposes this evil and unequivocally reveals violence as the heart and soul

---

3. Epistle to Diognetus 7:4, my translation.

of all human religion and culture. Once we grasp this, we can see that the death of Jesus was not a sacrificial transaction between an angry God and a willing divine sacrifice. The Father is a God of Life and would not wish death upon anyone, especially his beloved Son. But we did. And now we are revealed as the species that uses scapegoats to maintain our group identities. In other words, we are death dealers, not God.

Just as Abraham brought Isaac, so the Father brought the Son to the altar of our religion, our need for blood. We humans had over a long, long period of thousands of millennia learned that when we experienced social crisis nothing worked better than human sacrifice. It may be noted that today human sacrifice is banned everywhere on the planet. Why is that? Is it because we somehow outgrew it? No. It is the result of the power of the gospel to lift up the value of human life and the precious character of every human being. For two thousand years the passion of Jesus has been preached from pulpits around the world every Sunday. That's a lot of Sundays over a lot of millennia from a shit-ton of pulpits. And whether the gospel has been preached well or a bowdlerized sacrificial version has been preached, still it has had its effects on global culture. Even those who deny the existence of Jesus or are staunch atheists must reckon with the effects of the gospel on human culture.

It has been important to try and demonstrate several very important things when it comes to the Bible.

The first is that the Bible contains two streams, religion and revelation, and these streams do not run between the testaments but through them. Further these two streams have different voices; that of vengeance and that of forgiveness and mercy.

The second is that these streams are understood in terms of that which makes religion religion, namely sacrifice and blood; and that which makes revelation revelation, pure gracious forgiveness and love. Recognizing this is an insight from which there is no returning. It is a paradigm shift.

Third, I have argued that the early Christian heretics as well as the early church fathers really struggled with the question of the violence of God in the Jewish Scriptures, but ultimately both came up with solutions that were neither coherent or consistent.

Fourth, learning to read the Bible this way only energizes the great dogmas of Christendom. Far from leaving orthodoxy behind, an anthropological reading not only affirms things like the doctrine of the trinity, or Jesus as the divine-human mediator or even of Scripture as being revelatory, it also opens the way for us to live in relationships in a totally new and life-giving way.

If you expect the Bible to be perfect before you are able to say there is any revelation you will be sadly disappointed because you are asking Holy Scripture to perform a function it was never meant to have: belief in the Bible cannot be a substitute for trusting the Father. Protestant Christianity, particularly Calvinism, places trust in the Bible above trust in God. You can see this in the thousands of books devoted to explaining the "apparent" contradictions of the Bible. These cheap apologetics easily suck in the unwary whose newfound joyous faith is justified because they trust what is being said about The Book.

These apologetics diminish Holy Scripture by turning the text of the Bible into the "kurios" (LORD). This sleight-of-hand substitution of Scripture for the Living "kurios" Jesus Christ is the bane of Protestantism. Roman Catholicism substituted the papacy for the "kurios" and Orthodoxy has substituted the tradition for the "kurios." In fact, almost everywhere in Christendom one can find Jesus being displaced as the revelation of the Father. This displacement is why and how Christianity became so sacrificial. With a religious or sacrificial reading of the Bible the people can be kept in perpetual fear of a sacrificial God, and thus ensure that the church and its ministry (*sic*) flourish.

One of the premier messages of the gospel is that the good news about the character of God removes our fear of God. "Perfect love casts out fear."[4] The good news also removes our fear of death for we know there is no retribution coming our way in the afterlife. There may well be a reckoning where we have to learn to tell the truth about ourselves, but it will be a merciful reckoning, one which heals and restores.

If the gospel were about a Janus-faced "God" then it would be appropriate to present the alternatives of heaven and hell when one died. One could justify, as did Augustine in the early fifth century, that it is better to persecute and torture someone to "confess Christ" than to see them burn in the hereafter. One could go on to justify all manner of exploitation, colonization, and totalitarianism replete with the "enemy other" time and again, century after century, by appealing to the "just" or "powerful" God as the Divine Sovereign.

Thankfully, we now know better than that. We have had our eyes opened to just how vile religion can be, from justifying and hiding abuse to

---

4. 1 John 4:18.

pogroms against people groups. The Christian religion is not exempt from this and stands horridly out as a significant contributor to the pain of the world for the past two thousand years. There are those who see Christian history or the history of Christianity as "evil" in itself.

What was supposed to be good news was quickly turned into the same old bad news of all the other gods of other religions. And yet, conversely at the same time, we find the transformational thinking of the gospel breaking through in all manner of ways, in the early Christian care for the poor and the widow, the crashing of the patriarchal ceiling in some traditions where women were priests and prophetesses, and certain areas where slaves became bishops. We would be wrong to demand that these early Christians see everything at once. They, like us, are people of their time.

How much of our theology will be weighed in the balance and found lacking by our children and our grandchildren? When we come to deal with figures and movements of the past we should not expect them to think like we do; we must let each writer or poet or theologian or mystic be a person of their time and be diligent to look for whatever contributions they may have made. We would want the same historical mercy shown to us would we not?

So it is, we begin with the doctrine of the Trinity where anything we say about the Son can be said of the Father. We have inherited this from the apostolic church, and it was a clarion call over the next two hundred years. God is not to be divided into persons, attributes, roles, or modes. To speak of God revealing God's self is to claim that when God is revealed to us it is an indication that we are forgiven and our relationship restored.

By now you may realize that this book is to be read like peeling an onion. Just as I sought to head off at the pass any criticism that my approach is Marcionite, so now I must show that the Trinity as a doctrine is also a hermeneutic, a method of interpretation, a lens or a pair of glasses by which we read and comprehend what the Living God is saying to us by the Spirit.

The first thing I would say is that the doctrine of the Trinity is the way the Christian church frames our understanding of God. Notice I used the word "frames." A frame is the structure, but it is not the house. The wisest in the history of Christianity have always known this. The term they use with reference to this is "ineffable" which means that which cannot be described with words or is indescribable. Words or language, the frame of the house, will only take you so far. Fools reduce their knowledge of God by thinking that language is a medium capable of bearing the infinity of the divine.

We humans created our gods when we ritualized the mechanism of generative mimetic scapegoating. This action, which in its repetition spawned first religion then culture, is where all human language originates. Language is bloody. This is why it is important for any discussion of language's capacity to carry revelation to have as its thought base the transformation of language in blood. Linguistics, or at least all Christian discourse, can only begin with the cross of Christ and the problem of its relation to sacrifice.

Second, having read and delved into both the patristic as well as the great twentieth-century writers on the Trinity, we noted several crucial elements of the way we measure the frame, the doctrine of the Trinity. Anyone can claim they are trinitarian because they believe God to be three persons but the same substance. However, what lies definitionally behind the words "person" and "substance" create all manner of problems which are adopted as solutions and warp the frame considerably. What is eventually erected is like something out of a Tim Burton movie. Trinitarian doctrines of God abound in popular Christianity, but they are cartoons.

The first measurement tool has already been stated: the death of Jesus. In other words, the Christian doctrine of God is developed with specific reference to Jesus's passion. Paul and the writer of the Fourth Gospel insist that the Father was actively engaged in the death of Jesus "reconciling." For the writer of the Fourth Gospel, the giving of the Spirit is intimately tied with the death of Jesus as Paraclete, defender of victims. The three modes, or words by which the Christian describes God—Abba, Jesus, Spirit—make no sense if they do not begin here. If these words take their definition from anywhere else, be it from holy writings or human philosophy or science, then they have no connection with the God being described during the passion of Jesus. A doctrine of the Trinity that cannot withstand the hell of Golgotha is not worthy of consideration.

The second tool by which to measure a stable, and I would claim, orthodox doctrine of the Trinity is to ask about the role "economies of exchange" play. An economy of exchange is any relationship that is reciprocal; one gives in order to receive. This most ancient way of relating, from archaic potlatches to contemporary Christmas parties, has to do with the exchange of gifts. Life is all about exchange. You exchange your time for a paycheck which you exchange for cash which you exchange for goods and services. We are so culturally embedded in economies of exchange we cannot see the forest for the trees. Our religion is replete with it. God must have something from us in order to relate to us whether it is good works, obedience, faith, whatever. God needs something from us in order to give to us.

Economies of exchange were born in the process of humans learning to substitute the one for the many, that is, what Girard calls the victimage mechanism or scapegoating.[5] Human life, in its broken, bent or "fallen" state is lived in the Matrix of Exchange. If you have any view of an economy of exchange in your theology (or what J. B. Torrance has identified as a "contract" theology)[6] you cannot speak of grace, unmerited or freely given. This is where the principle of a "theology of the cross" is juxtaposed to the problem of economies of exchange and becomes the solution of grace.

God did not theoretically reconcile the creation and all humanity back to God's self, God actually reconciled all things, on earth and in heaven (so to speak). This is simply a fact. Reconciliation is a done deal, once for all. Period. End of sentence. Mic Drop. God did what God did because of who God is; God's character in the drama of human history, in the figure of Jesus of Nazareth, is where economies of exchange were challenged at every level, political ("You shall not rule as the gentiles"), ethics ("give to the poor"), economics ("sell all you have" [and note Jesus apparently did not carry money]), theology ("God makes sun and rain for both good and evil"), religious ("mercy is better than sacrifice" and the prophetic act in the temple), etc. The entirety of the life of Jesus is against our human orientation to relating through the mechanism of an economy of exchange.

A healthy doctrine of the Trinity has no economy of exchange. God is love. God is not love and something else. God is light. God is not light and darkness. In short God is not Janus-faced. God is gracious and merciful and loving and gentle and kind because that is who God is in God's self. God is not different in God's self than God is toward humanity at Calvary. All that needs to be said and can be said about the character of God can only be done in Calvary's light. Jesus's death is the revelation by which all things are brought to light.

This is where PSA advocates have turned the gospel of Jesus into its very antithesis and thus created Christian myth. Their understanding of Calvary is replete with economies of exchange and so they must read Jesus's death through a sacrificial lens, justifying once again that old serpent, the mechanism of sacred violence. One must say that their god is an ugly God, not worthy of being compared to the Abba of Jesus. Their god is no different

---

5. Girard, *Things Hidden from the Foundation of the World*, part 1.
6. Torrance, "Covenant or Contract?"

than all the other gods who require sacrifice. This view of "god" is the most pagan one of all. It has completely taken the very story which deconstructs the Janus-faced god and economies of exchange and made that god into the image and likeness of all gods of sacred violence. Protestants have yet to discover the gospel!

Third, a healthy, robust, and orthodox doctrine of the Trinity has made the "shift to relationality." Many are the secular disciplines which conceive of "reality" and "person" as relational, from physics and cosmology to biology and ecosystems, to linguistics and semiotics, to sociology and anthropology, to the cognitive sciences, to philosophy and economics, political theory and psychology (systems theory) to gaming and computer simulation. The twentieth century saw a profound and deep shift to being-as-relation all across the frame of human knowledge.

Much of the older language of the doctrine of the Trinity as it is used in the West stumbles because it is seeking to do two things: the first misstep seeks to relate non-created being to that which is created in philosophical language, and second, it has the unfortunate merit of having to understand the Trinity as "*personae*," thus requiring each "person" of the Trinity to be a self-autonomous being, yet somehow all one in substance (*ousia, substantia*). The vast majority of clergy and laity thus come to the doctrine of the Trinity, can't make heads or tails of it, and so ignore or dismiss it. Those who do show an interest just gum it up for failure to bring the doctrine under the critical control of the cross.

If "being" is in fact "being-in-relation," if there is nothing autonomous, if humans are not islands making social contracts, if all reality is related on the quantum or string theory level, and if, with the great theologians of the twentieth century, we reconsider "person" as "being-in-relationship," the only way to speak of God is to speak relationally. This is just what the first Christians did and it has been rediscovered in our own time.

One of the crucial aspects of this last century's conversation on the Trinity can be highlighted from the work of Karl Barth. It has powerful ramifications on a number of levels. The first is that any talk about God apart from God's relation to humanity is speculative and idle talk. It is not gospel. Thus, Barth often faults Catholics and Protestant divines on the same score: they seek to speak of God apart from the way God has chosen to reveal God's self. Revelation is reconciliation in Barth and reconciliation is revelation!

The second implication of relationality is that rather than conceiving of God as three stages (as every form of dispensationalism does), that is sequentially, one, two, three, the term God is rather conceived of as a verb rather than a noun. The third implication is that all forms of heresy are rejected which assert that there is a God behind God. In classic theological language this is the separation of the "economic" Trinity (God as revealed in space, time, history) from the "ontological" Trinity (God in God's self). There is no hidden God or part of God or side of God or characteristic of God that is not revealed in Jesus. In Jesus we see the *holon* of God, but we see it always as relationality: Abba to Son and Spirit, Spirit to Abba and Son, Son to Abba and Spirit. This is the way Jesus speaks, and this is also the way Paul speaks. One could make a case that relationality suffuses the Johannine discourse about God as well.

Here are the necessary things one measures a healthy, strong and beautiful doctrine of the Trinity by:

- It begins and ends with Jesus's passion
- It rejects all economies of exchange (God is free, grace is the character of God)
- It provisionally thinks in "relational" categories and worldviews
- It understands the "person" in relational, vibrant, and dynamic terms

Now having said all of this, some might say that I have skirted the assignment to "explain the doctrine of the Trinity." The fact is that because I do not accept so many of the hidden premises and presuppositions, that is, the underlying definition of the average person's understanding of terms like "being," "substance," "nature," "person" etc., I cannot explain the doctrine of the Trinity for it needs no explaining. Only that which is unclear or off the mark needs "ex-plain-ing." God's self, revealed as "for us" (*hyper humon*) in the life and death of Jesus of Nazareth is crystal clear. God is experienced as Abba-Source, Son-History, and Spirit-Existential Awareness, all of which are one and the same reality. However, the Christian experience of God is going to center on the middle term, Son-history, in order to understand and know Abba-Source and Spirit-Existential Awareness. In short, a doctrine of the Trinity, or a doctrine of God shorn of the humanity of Jesus and thus the redemption of our humanity, is no doctrine of God; and further a Christology or any form of the telling of the life and teaching of Jesus which is not cruciform is no Christology at all.

The vibrant, healthy, life-giving doctrine of the Trinity is beautiful. There is so much one could say about a doctrine of the Trinity, but my response to the quest to "explain the Trinity" has to be, "let's redefine the terms in light of all we know to be true scientifically rather than remain in the quagmire of Greek psychology and philosophy." If you are willing to do that hard work then we can have a conversation; if not, well, best of luck with your Burtonesque doctrine of God!

One final element presents itself to us. If it is the case that religion and revelation are both contained in Scripture and must be distinguished, it cannot be said that the "God" of the Old Testament is an ogre, and the "God" of the New Testament is love. Revelation is a process that takes place at the very heart of religion, which is sacrifice. This is why the Bible is so keen on the sacrificial process. This is also why we not only find that move away from myth to be incomplete in the Jewish Scriptures, but we also can show how the revelation of the Father in the Son by the Spirit was turned into a religion. There are sacrificial elements in both Testaments. There is also revelation shot through both Testaments. It is revelation, specifically the revelation of the love of the Father in the dying Jesus, that allows us to discriminate between them.

There is a heresy to be avoided at all costs: that of supersessionism. This view is found in theology wherever the church replaces Israel, or the New Testament supplants the Jewish Scriptures. We find this to be abhorrent because it fails to take the active role of the revealing God in Jewish history seriously. It also assumes that Christianity is the "perfect" revelation. It isn't. No appeal to an infallible institution or book or interpreter works anymore. The evidence is preponderantly against such a view, although weaker minded persons will still seek such.

While we recognize that the event of Jesus Christ is the pinnacle, the fullness, the wholeness of the revelation of the Father, the early church made the mistake of assuming that the Jewish Scriptures, when they talked about God, were automatically talking about the Father of Jesus. This is especially true from the mid-second century onward, but it can also be found in some New Testament literature. How else shall we explain the enormous gulf between the apostle Paul and Jerusalem Christianity? These seismic differences between Paul and the apostles in the Jerusalem church are somehow largely overlooked or ignored from the pulpit of the Protestant Christian church, leaving many who rely solely upon them for their theological education failing to recognize that they even existed. But exist they did, spanning the nature of the Law, the nature of the gospel, and the mission to the gentiles. I think it is fair to say that most early apostolic Christianity did not allow the revelation in Jesus Christ to penetrate their view of God, at least not completely. As noted below, Paul himself underwent a huge change in his own positions on such matters between the time of his letters to Thessalonica and his latter epistles as, over time, his encounter with the true gospel penetrated his heart and mind and transformed his thinking.

There are several observations one can make about the literature influenced by early Jewish (Jerusalem church–oriented) Christianity. Those books still tend to retain some sort of bad ending for many. For example, Matthew's Gospel has a number of "Gehenna" sayings not found in Mark or Luke and which can arguably be traced to the author. The ending of the Johannine Apocalypse is well known with its Judgment scene and fiery ending for many. This same eschatology (view of the end times) can even be found in Paul in his earliest letters to the Thessalonians (composed circa 41 CE). It would appear that in his later authentic letters he has abandoned this eschatology for a more hopeful vision such as we see at the end of Rom 11, 1 Cor 15, 2 Cor 5, or in Ephesians.

A second marker of religion is the express use of sacrificial language. This can be seen when an author understands the divine-human relationship in transactional terms. This is most easily seen in prayers where we promise to do something for "God" hoping to receive our request in return. There are no atheists in foxholes! Religion is always transactional; it is an I-give-in-order-to-receive mentality. The same can be seen when we think God says, "Do this and you will be rewarded, do that and you will be punished." Religion has been from the beginning a transaction between humanity and divinity.

This transactional thinking has two significant moments in Christian theology: in atonement and eschatology. In eschatology, as we have said, there is a judgment scene with dispensed rewards and punishments. In atonement this is manifested as a theory of salvation made between the Father and the Son whereby the Son would pay the debt for our sin to the Father's holiness and so assuage God's anger. Protestant orthodoxy (*sic*) calls both of these "good news," but there is nothing good about either of them.

The Bible gives us different atonement theories and varied eschatologies. We should not be surprised at this. The biblical writers all had some relationship to religion and revelation, and some saw more clearly than others. By understanding how to know God as Trinity in the light of the cross of Jesus, we have a true metric to discriminate between the false character of religion and sacrifice and the truth of revelation which leads to life and peace.

The alternative to this is to see that in the Gospel, there is this thing called *charis*. Now charis is not transactional. God as charis-acting is not in response to anything we may say or need or want. It is grounded in the love that God has for us as his children, his creation. Charis is free, unconditioned and unconditional. Love loves because love is love; it can do no other. This is not at all a kind of love we humans know. In each of our relationships we like or love someone because . . . reasons. That is, we like or love someone as they fulfill their part of the transaction in our relationship by liking us or loving us in return. As soon as the transactional character of the relationship changes, as soon as someone is "owed" more than the other then there are problems. Charis as agape ("grace as love") has no economy of exchange like religion.

This is not so in our relation to the Father. Our redemption is freely proffered. It is a total gift and it requires nothing but trust: trust that we are loved, trust that circumstances are not a metric of divine love, trust that the Father will create meaning for our lives. These are the behaviors Jesus displayed as he was crucified. He trusted his Father for all things and knew his Father would hear his prayers because he was loved by the Father unconditionally.

A third marker of religion has to do with having correct knowledge. I am not disparaging knowledge or knowing, however, following the great Swiss theologian Karl Barth, I acknowledge that "trust" has its own inherent knowledge that it is working out. Scholars might say that "trust" (*pistis*) has its own epistemology and hermeneutic. What they mean is that the act of trusting the Father, that what is said in the good news about God is true and trustworthy, brings with it its own reasoning and interpretive process. This means that we cannot come to the gospel with our own current ways of deciding between true and false, or with questions like "How do we know what we know?" We must leave behind ideas about what the world is, let alone what a "God" is. The gospel changes not just what we think but more importantly how we think.

Sadly, most people who have undergone some process of deconstruction do not realize this. They bring their old, tired questions about God and evil, history and time, spirit and matter to a message that asks them to drop these questions and learn to ask different ones. My students will tell you that I am constantly reminding them to question their questions. If you ask the wrong question you are guaranteed to get the wrong answer. It is always good to ask if the questions we are asking are the same questions that are put to us in the gospel. If we are honest, we will find that most of the time we have been asking the wrong questions. And we wonder why our faith doesn't work! How can it work if we have not yet learned to see the world through the lens of the gospel which, as I said, creates its own distinct way of knowing?

The gospel way of knowing does not begin from a position outside the problem, as though we were objective observers; rather, because it begins in trust, it places us squarely in the middle of a relational experience with divinity, specifically with a divinity so beautiful, so bountiful, so loving, so merciful that we can know "God" and call upon "God" as a child does a parent. Trust. From this starting point, we can then live into that which we experience, and as we read the Gospels and learn about Jesus and his background, we can begin to see the pattern of life that he lived, and that we too can live. This pattern is called "discipleship," and while we shall have some things to say about this in the last chapter, the companion volume in this series will explore this in depth as we explore the Sermon on the Mount (Matt 5–7).

Our experience is not willy-nilly though. It is the concrete experience of trusting in times both light and dark, when seasons are plentiful and when they are impoverished. Trust is learning to be grateful in all situations, not just the best of them. It is the hard times, the dark nights, the grief and loss journeys of our souls where we truly learn who the Father is. It is when we should feel utterly abandoned that we find ourselves wrapped in a cocoon of love. Admittedly this is not the experience of the many. Why is this?

At first, we navigate these dark times with little trust and a bazillion questions. As they repeat, we begin to doubt the very existence of God. Most people end up here and spend the rest of their lives here. We were meant for more than that. Crucifixion of the soul and the death of the body were never meant to be last words. No. Resurrection, life, and peace are the final words, and it is in this we trust and place our hope. When you surrender your questions during a dark night of the soul and learn to trust that you are loved and that your circumstances do not indicate anything about the love of God for you, you will find the peace that comes with the gospel. It is this trusting process that we are called to nurture the entirety of our Christian life.

Theology is what happens when we take this cruciform experience of the Trinity into the intellect. The Father revealed in the Son historically, and the Son revealed in us existentially by the Son-shaped Spirit of the Father, is the space from which we begin our talk about God. We bear witness to this God when we recognize and affirm that Jesus of Nazareth indeed showed us the character of the Father, and especially demonstrated the depth of the Father's love in sending Jesus into our world, himself experiencing these dark nights of the soul and growing in trust, even as we do.

Theology is not correct doctrine. May God deliver us from this way of thinking. There is not a single theology on the planet that is so internally self-consistent that one could say it is through and through "correct doctrine." I have found myself going through constant changes in my own theology (as did the apostle Paul). I have never left the great Christian doctrines, but I have learned that these doctrines need to be seen in the light of the gospel rather than the other way around. Healthy doctrine develops organically. The seed becomes the stalk that bursts the soil, then the full-grown plant. The plant and the seed are different in form, but they are the same in substance. One grows apples from apple seeds. No one plants apple seeds expecting to grow oranges. In the same way the great doctrines of the Trinity, the life, death, and resurrection of Jesus, the coming of the Holy Spirit and how it all works out in the end are there in seed form in the apostolic Scriptures. And for almost two thousand years we have been seeking to get oranges from the apple seeds planted by early Christianity.

Why is this? There are many reasons I could give, but I would like to single out a basic, primary, fundamental mistake that early Christianity made, and this can be seen in the shift away from "trust" to "correct doctrine." This move is known as "Gnosticism," the belief that correct knowledge saves us. Early Christian gnostics proliferated like rabbits in the second century. Whether one was in Rome, Alexandria, or Ephesus, there were plenty of teachers who were there to tell you they had it all figured out and that their theology was true, correct and proper. The (so-called) "orthodox" church fathers spent considerable energies combatting Gnosticism. Thinkers like Justin Martyr, Irenaeus, and Augustine thought they were creating an orthodox theology when they countered the gnostic teachers. The problem is that rather than question whether gnostic theological questions were even real, they entertained them. Christian Gnosticism was never touched by a theology of the cross, and so it also failed to allow God as self-revealing Trinity to reframe their view of divinity or counter their dualism.

The theological decisions the church fathers made at this time arguing against Gnosticism, some for good and some for ill, paved the way for Christianity to spend its entire historical two thousand-year life battling Gnosticism. It is our battle today. How many have you known who have claimed to know "the truth," whether it be "the truth" of their experience, or of some alleged way to read the Bible or of some institution or tradition?

Gnosticism is the persistent and perennial heresy that confronts every Christian generation. By replacing trust with knowledge, Christian Gnosticism removes the beneficent relation established in the gospel between God and us and replaces it with having correct knowledge about this God; and such knowledge presupposes the category of "god" rather than letting the gospel redefine that category. And so it is, we bring in the back door what the gospel has kicked out of the front door: the presuppositions, assumptions, and questions we thought were real: our understanding of divinity, humanity, life and history, evil and good.

When knowledge or reason reign supreme what is sought is the ground of that knowledge. How do we know what we know? What is the thinking process? What is the ground or basis for what we think and say? And so, we drill down using tools like philosophy, linguistics, history, and other disciplines so we can get to the bottom of why we believe this or that, or why we believe anything at all. The further we go the more we ask, "how do I know this is true or that is real?" and we fail to realize we have dived so deep that there is no more sunlight. We are just surrounded by the inky blackness and great depths of our intellectual conundrums. Our questions have become burdens, and in some cases, they have become taskmasters. Either way we lose. This is the way of Gnosticism. The gnostic god does not exist and so the gnostic god cannot answer our questions. Idols are mute, deaf and blind. People think that rejecting this god makes them atheists. It does! And it will debilitate some who will remain with their unanswered, unanswerable questions. But it will motivate others to ask if there is any good news, any good god behind all of the human theologies and religions. They seek the unknown god (Acts 17). The good news is that the unknown god has revealed God's self with a name: Jesus. It is him and his way, his message, his pattern of life, that we trust.

The way of trust is so very different. Knowledge that arises from the trust relation established in the gospel retains its focus on that which makes the Good News good news indeed, namely that the Father is not like any of our gods. The Father has no dark side, no shadow of turning, no mysterious side for us to load with theological baggage. The Father does not create suffering or death as we understand them. We perceive suffering and death as evil or bad. Suffering and death are about change and transformation, and as such are built into the universe.

When we feel that our lives are soul crushing, and we try to understand them from the perspective of religion, we can only feel badly for ourselves and either hate God or quit believing. But when we know that life is about constant change and adaptation, when we trust that these soul-crushing challenges of life are there for our benefit, for our transformation, and that "God makes all things work together for good to those that love him and are called for his purpose";[7] we can let go of the hurt, the pain, the nightmares that beset us.

Life is the same for those who trust and for those who don't trust. Life is unfair to both; life is ambiguous for both. How those who trust in the Father, revealed in the Son by the Spirit, react to such life struggles is very different from those who have no trust. We are those who are able to continue smiling, knowing that today's struggles are just for today. Tomorrow may bring more of the same, but we will cross that bridge when we awaken. For today, we give thanks and live in peace. Knowledge cannot bring this kind of peace, only trust does.

By now we have learned the importance of discerning the difference between religion and revelation. We have seen the value of asking the better questions and have sought to understand how to retain the value of the biblical writings for our theology. We have negated any notion of a relationship between the writers and some kind of dictation theory or inerrancy and God. We have seen that the revelation of God's self in Jesus Christ and the message carried about him by the Holy Spirit brings us into relation with this very God and creates trust. It is trustworthy to say the Father is good, the Father is Light, the Father is Love, the Father is mercy, the Father is grace personified. Doctrines or views of God that bring the Father into conjunction with anger, violence, and death are nothing more than Christian religion and are not worthy of our trust. How can you trust a god who is now loving, then hateful, now jealous, then caring, now judgmental and holy, then merciful and forgiving? What must one do to make sure one was

---

7. Rom 8:28.

on the right side of this God? How is one ever supposed to know deep in one's soul that one is truly loved by such a Janus-faced deity?

The implications of this are staggering. When we separate the God and Father of Jesus Christ from the Janus-faced gods of human religion we are "hallowing God's name." We are living the prayer we were taught to pray. The Father is not at all like our gods. The Christian god has come under fire since the twelfth century. Criticism reared its head in the fifteenth century and a scathing dam of it burst in the seventeenth century. Ever since that time, over and over again, thinkers both Christian and non-Christian have sought to differentiate what they were hearing in the gospel from the Christian religion. Here in our time, at the end of Christendom and the beginning of this next historical period (Transhumanism), it is essential for Christians to understand that the gods of sacred violence are nothing more than satans clothed in light (more on this in the next chapter).

I remind the reader that in discovering this we have not fallen into any old or new heresy. We have taken with utmost seriousness the great doctrines of Christianity. But we have learned to discuss them from a different perspective, that of the message of the gospel of, and about, Jesus Christ crucified. The Christian tradition, like its religious birth mother Judaism, has a treasure trove of wisdom, insight, and life-giving advice. We are not throwing out the Christian religion like so many deconstructors; but we are distinguishing that which is religion from that which is revelation within it.

There might be some who will say we are twisting Scripture; if so, we are twisting it the same way Jesus, Luke, Paul, and the writer to the Fourth Gospel did. In my book *The Jesus Driven Life*, I offer many examples of this. There I noted that there was no such thing as a "Bible" in first-century Judaism. Different groups held different writings sacred. There were many versions of the same text, and the text was itself translated into different languages. Jesus and Paul can easily quote their "canonical" texts and add, omit, or even change things just as the Septuagint or Targumic translators did. The text was not so sacred that it was venerated as is found in conservative Protestant Christianity today. Back then, with no official canon and different groups holding to different authoritative texts with different methods for interpreting those texts, there developed a great fluidity in Judaism and interpretation of traditions, oral and textual. We can see this in the debates in both the Christian New Testament and the Mishnah of Judaism (circa 200).

It is this great debate about the character of God that we are invited to participate in when we pick up a Bible to read it. We do the Bible a complete and total injustice when we read it expecting God to "speak to us." We do the concept of canon a complete disservice when we cavalierly assume that the Bible has one author, God. Some, even though they may recognize that there are difficulties in Scripture, act as though the difficulties are their problem not God's. They spend an inordinate amount of energy trying to harmonize that which cannot be harmonized, that is, violence and the sacred. In Jesus Christ these two were forever sundered and it is our place to learn Christian theology anew from this starting point.

In order to do that we must ask what is really being demystified in the gospel of the crucified Christ. So far, we have discerned that human understanding of divinity is false, it is a lie. What is being demystified in the gospel is more than this though. The gospel of the cross of Jesus Christ tackles the thorniest and most difficult questions of all, including that of evil. And it does so in a way that is shocking, liberating, and stunning all at the same time. To this we turn now.

# 4

# The Devil

There is a saying that has traveled around Evangelical circles ever since I was a young man. I don't know where it originated but it goes something like this: the greatest thing the devil has ever done is to convince us he doesn't exist. Those who do not believe in a devil have evidently been seduced by the dark side. I would like to counter this and say that the greatest effect of the original liar was to convince us that he does exist. Now you may notice a paradox here: I am asserting both the existence of an original liar and also claiming that he doesn't exist. Both are true. I would contend that the paramount deception of "the devil" is not so much to convince us that he doesn't exist, but rather to convince us that the form we think he exists in is real. Herein lies the problem of evil that we shall examine.

Whether we were raised Christian or entered into it at a later age, we were all taught a narrative about the devil. That story could be influenced by Hollywood, medieval superstition, and ancient literature not found in the Bible. In the past decades there has been a plethora of books written on the devil/satan. All of them tell basically the same story because the devil is an idea before anything else. We have talked about Janus-faced gods in earlier chapters. These are the earliest gods we know (and since then, the only gods we are familiar with). The origins of religion are shrouded in the dim mists of our human pre-history, but the story of the devil has an actual beginning: tenth to seventh-century BCE Persia! In an attempt to make sense of all the gods, both good and evil, a religious prophet Zoroaster (Zarathustra) concluded that there were two divine beings, one good, the other evil. This theological dualism would penetrate every major world religion including Judaism, and through Judaism, Christianity.

It is important to know that the devil, as an idea, will change over time and we can see that change as it occurs in the Bible. If we are willing to see the devil passages as an idea that develops, we can make better sense of what is happening than if we try to harmonize all the (alleged) texts that speak about this subject. So, for example, if we take Gen 3, and compare it to the prologue of Job and the book of Zechariah, we have two different stories. In the Gen 3 story there is a talking snake, not identified as a devil (this comes later in the apocryphal book of the Wisdom of Solomon around 200 BCE). It is only in literature produced after the return from the exile that we find a specific figure known as "the satan" as in Wisdom, the prologue to Job, and Zechariah. In Job and Zechariah, the satan is an adversarial figure of humanity whose role is to prosecute sinners and turn them over to "God" for divine justice. This is how the satan becomes known as "the accuser," a label given him by the author of Revelation.

Then of course there is the well-known story of the origin of the devil, an angel of light, who leads an army of angels to rebel against God, loses, and is cast out of heaven, in some stories to earth, in some to outer darkness and in some to Hades/"Hell." No matter where he is exiled, the satan still has some power here in the earthly sphere, earning him the title "the prince of the power of the age" or "the prince of this age." In the story of the Watchers in 1 Enoch (1–36), after the battle in heaven, there is a negotiation whereby the leadership of the angelic rebellion asks for 10 percent of the demonic army to be left behind on earth, a request to which God acquiesces!

For half a century prior to the New Testament the devil became the one to blame for evil in the world. He (generic use of the pronoun) is responsible for deception and death. The worldview of 1 Enoch would come to dominate all other understandings of the devil. It is possible that Isa 45 is a reaction against this too strong a view of the devil as the evil counterpart to the divine good. The author even attributes the creation of evil to God to demonstrate that there is only one God who is sovereign over all life. The author of Isaiah would be affirming total monotheism with no other gods, good or evil. Evil is not a god.

In the first century CE, the time of Jesus and the apostolic church, the 1 Enoch story would have been fairly well known, especially among the Essenes. John the Baptist and Jesus were certainly familiar with it, as was the writer of Jude and the Revelator. Paul, I think, does not share this viewpoint (except for his two early letters to the Thessalonians), and the writer of the Fourth Gospel refers not to 1 Enoch but the Torah narrative (Gen 3). It can be argued that the writer of the Gospel of Mark has couched Jesus's ministry in the antique archetype of the battle of the dragon, or Leviathan. Jesus's ministry in Mark is a cosmic battle between God and the satan. In Luke the demonic is presupposed, but we are given no clue that 1 Enoch has influenced this writer. Finally, there is some scholarly literature suggesting that Matthew's Gospel was composed to counter this narrative of Enoch. No matter how we slice or dice it, the battle between good and evil, light and darkness, run rampant through the New Testament, but it is not the same story line as we find in other speculations about the devil.

The Bible gives us three possible ways to talk about the devil/satan.

1. God created evil. Isa 45:7: "I form the light, and create darkness; I make peace, and create evil; I am the LORD, that doeth all these things." In this view, God is the author of both light and darkness, good and evil. God is both a cursing and blessing God. The problem with this view is that God is ultimately Janus-faced. The New Testament response to this is to say that "God is love" and "God is light" (1 John), or that "in God there is no dark side [no shadow of turning]" (James). If one believes that God's character is fully and truly revealed in Jesus, then one must reject Isaiah's way of understanding God.

2. The way around this is to say that God makes all things "good" (Gen 1) but that good became evil. This is what the watcher myth or apocalyptic literature of Second Temple Judaism did. In this view, the devil is a good angel who rebels, is cast from heaven, and then wreaks havoc on humanity. Some cite Isa 14 or Ezek 28 to justify this view canonically but there are several problems with this. First, Isaiah and Ezekiel are referencing human kings. Second, the satan plays only a marginal role in Jewish thinking about evil prior to apocalyptic literature (arising in the third century BCE). The problem here is that the satan must be conceived in the realm of the transcendent outside humanity. The satan becomes an "almost divine" type of figure in this scenario. One solution was that of the author of the prologue of Job, who places the satan among the divine court as a prosecuting attorney akin to The Grand Inquisitor. Another was that of the apocalyptists. Neither is satisfactory.

3. A third possibility is that evil does not arise from without but from within the human condition. Early Jewish proto-rabbis came up with this idea. Indeed, the priest who composed the second creation narrative (commonly known as the Yahwist) had incredible insight which Paul reflects in Rom 7 and James in Jas 1: that God created humans with two "impulses" or "yetzerim," one good the other evil. Think of those pictures where humans have a devil on one shoulder and an angel on the other. Jesus may (and I say "may") have been alluding to this in the Lord's Prayer when he said, "Deliver us from [the] evil [impulse]."

The New Testament story line encompasses the demise of the devil, or the conquering of the evil, or the casting out of the satan. The New Testament is the story of the end of the devil and his machinations. It is not concerned about the origin of evil, nor does it spend any time there. For the apostolic church the only reason to mention the devil at all was to speak of his dethronement. If the devil is an idea that develops, we must ask three questions: Is the devil a person? Is the devil real? And how is the devil overcome?

For most Christians, the satan is a malevolent person just like they are but without a human body. This begs the all-important question: what is a person? How do you define what constitutes a person? What is personality? Before you continue, take a moment and write down your response to this question. This is an important exercise. Go ahead. Stop and consider, "what is a person?"

Most of us tend to think of people as agents of independent moral authority, that persons are those that can choose or have so-called "free-will." The concept of personality, however, is far more complex than that. Even if we say that a person is an autonomous moral agent possessing free will, we then need to define free will. What is will? What makes it free? Further yet, we have to define the terms that we use when it comes to our definition of free will. The problem here is that once we go down this road we leave all knowledge gained from the human sciences behind, simply speculating and creating a view of "person" far more indebted to our presuppositions than to what we actually know about people.

Particularly since the Enlightenment (ca. 1800), we have been taught that people are autonomous moral agents, that we all stand alone, and that we are all responsible for our own choices. In the last one hundred years however, there has been a move away from this way of thought, recognizing that the concept of "personhood" requires redefinition. We are no longer to be conceived of as "free moral agents" who make choices determined by our own individual wills. Relationality is now the watchword when it comes to understanding what it means to be "persons." Speaking of humans, we are beings-in-relationships.

Our identity comes not from some isolated thing in each of us, but from our relationships. So, e.g., there is no such thing as Michael Hardin. Who "I" am is the confluence of all my relationships. Take away my relationships and "I" do not exist. "I" am my relationships. We are not individuals, lonely islands just bumping each other from time to time in the sea of life. To use a term coined by René Girard, we are "interdividuals." As long as we understand personhood as discrete individual entities, each with their own will, rationality, and ability to choose, we will remain mired in discussions that are little more than speculative quagmires. Scientific research in social psychology and into the human brain has demonstrated that we are in deep structural relationship with one another well beyond the conscious level. We are interdependent beings.

Our choices do not come from within but from without inasmuch as our desires, which we perceive to arise from within ourselves, are actually experienced internally even though they are externally derived. What we want to call our "own" desires/wants, are in reality the non-conscious taking up of the desires of others and making them our own. This is a huge shift. We want to believe that our desires are our own. Learning that all wants/desires are non-consciously socially mediated and appropriated is hard. This kind of self-examination will take you to your deepest core, where you will find that your entire self is an illusion. You are a social construct. Even the way you tell the story of your life has been mediated through cultural values and norms.

For many people this will prove troublesome. We can be stubborn when it comes to protecting the integrity of our ego. However, I would rather have a definition of "person" that has some grounding in reality (that which is scientifically demonstrable), not pure speculation. So, as we consider what it means for the satan to be a "person," it is important to remember that our worldviews will determine how we understand this and what we bring to the table in our definition of "personhood." Would you rather just speculate as to what a "person" is, or would you prefer to take advantage of all the wealth of accumulated science (disciplines in the humanities include, but are not limited to anthropology and its subdisciplines psychology, sociology, neuroscience, quantum physics, evolutionary development, the science of religion, game theory, child development, mathematics, literary theory) that has helped us to see ourselves not as islands on the ocean, but as part of an inner connected reality? We will do the latter, and by reframing our definition of "person," we will come to see that the satan is not a person in the older sense of an autonomous, good, free moral agent turned evil, but that the satan is bound up intimately with what it means to be persons-in-relationships.

It is the Torah story that gives us this clue: the snake is also in the garden with the man and the woman. A snake that talks? We are obviously dealing with the category of myth and to read the text literally would be absurd for snakes don't talk. But myth is a fine category to use when discussing the origin of things. This is what myths seek to be: originary stories.

If we are willing to acknowledge that the fallen angel myth of 1 Enoch is not part of the Old Testament idea of the origin of evil then it is possible to read Gen 2–4 in a different light. The reading I am proposing is an anthropological one. Let me explain what I mean. Rather than come to this text burdened with a host of assumptions about how the text was formed or who wrote it, or how it was inspired or if it is inspired, I will interpret this text for what insight it may offer about the human condition. What it says about God or spiritual matters is an irrelevance to me at this juncture; right now, I seek to discern how the text "reads me" as a human being. One further note: we need to come at this text as though the concept of "The Fall" had never entered our mind, as though Plato, Augustine, Calvin, and almost two millennia of the (Western) Christian doctrine of original sin had never existed. We want to read this text pretending we have never read it before and that there is no such thing as a God. This is not blasphemy, but it may be the only way some have of learning how to see this text in a new and liberating light.

First things first. There are no such things as talking snakes, so we know we are dealing with something metaphorical, something symbolic. Second, we can immediately recognize that it is an "originary myth," it is a story about the origins of the world and the human being, similar to other types of stories/myths found all over the planet. So now we know how to classify it and what it is seeking to communicate. Third, we see that it is the second of two creation myths, the first being Gen 1:1—2:4. We can see many of the subtle differences between the tales. You may notice that in the first creation story the male and female are created together (androgynously), while in the second creation myth they are created hierarchically; typically, the woman is taken from the male and seen as subservient. Yuck! I, and others, see the woman created last as the crown of creation.

As we read Gen 2–4, we notice that several words get repeated. Words like man, woman, eat, fruit, tree, Lord God, God, and of course, serpent. There is another word that appears once at the end of chapter 2 and twice in the first seven verses of chapter 3, or in other words, three times in eight verses; that word is "*arum.*" The first time "*arum*" appears is in 2:25, where "the man and his wife were both '*arum.*'" The second is in 3:1, where the "serpent was more '*arum*' than any other wild animal," and the last is in 3:8, where after having eaten of the fruit of the tree "then the eyes of both were opened and they knew that they were '*arum.*'" So, what is this *arum* business and why is this word used of both the human and the serpent? How can a word mean "naked" and "shrewd" or "clever"? Rather than go into deep, dark, technical places where horrendous etymological creatures wait to gobble up the weak and weary, I offer this simple example as a suggestion. The word "*arum*" is used in Gen 42:9 by Joseph who accuses his brothers of spying out "the nakedness of the land." That is, places where the land may well be vulnerable or penetrable to enemy attack. Ah-Ha! The snake has no defense mechanisms! It has no hands, feet or spine so it is vulnerable (although it may have a venomous tongue). *Arum* then is a word that connotes vulnerability. In the first use of the word, the male and the female had no idea that one could hurt the other, thus they were vulnerable and not existing in a place of shame (the feeling that would result from hurting the other who was vulnerable). The second time the word is used, it is in regard to the snake that is also the most vulnerable of any of the wild creatures, thus making the connection between the snake (mediated desire) and the humans: they are both *arum*. The third time the word is used, the couple have eaten of the fruit of the tree of the knowledge of good and evil and are aware that they can hurt one another and be hurt by the other, thus they begin "clothing themselves," that is, making themselves less vulnerable. To what are the couple and the snake both vulnerable? Shall we be content with *arum* referring to human genitalia inasmuch as they are exposed or vulnerable? How might this text be about core human identity (rather than sex, sexuality, or gender)? Let's get beyond Augustine and Freud into something new and insightful.

Let me recall where we are going with this: from a purely human perspective, the serpent is (represents) that part of the human which responds to the prohibition in Gen 2 not to eat of the tree of knowledge. We all know that when something is banned to us, we want it all the more. There is something seductive about the forbidden. So, we ought not to be surprised then when one part of the human reacts to the prohibition by questioning it. The human is the only animal that once its needs are satisfied, does not know what it wants. That is, humans experience a lack. This lack is the problem of desire. If you recall the emphasis about our *interdividuality*, that we are not isolated, but interconnected as a species, and if you recall that I have said that desire does not arise from within us but from without (that is, in relation to the other), and that this has been shown scientifically in studies in brain research (neurophysiology, neural networks, and mirror neurons), then it will not come as a surprise when I say that the serpent's engagement with the woman is a literary way of showing the true problem of the human condition: desire is easily corrupted.

That corruption can first of all be seen in the serpent's question "Did God say, 'You shall not eat from any tree in the garden?'" God did not say that. God prohibited only the one tree. The woman's response is a further distortion, for she adds to the command not to eat of the tree the further prohibition "nor touch it." The serpent compounds the deceit of desire by adding that the human, by eating of the tree will "become God-like," that is, that the human will have all ultimate desires met ("the desire for the being of the other—being like God"). The fact is that when the woman eats nothing happens. Her eyes are not opened, nor does she die. It is only after the man imitates the woman that consequences abound.

This text connects desire and imitation. Desire is mediated through the other. We want what others want, we value what others value, we take what others have thinking that in so doing we shall find fulfillment. The text shows that this is not the case, and that all we are left with when we imitate each other's desires is a sense of alienation. The man and woman immediately sensed alienation from God. When we don't get what we want we feel empty. We feel even alienated from ourselves. Note that the male is not absent from this scene of discourse between the serpent and the woman "for he was with her." All of this literarily suggests that the man, the woman and the serpent are one big figure of the process of mediated desire and its consequences. The origin of evil, the opening of the eyes to discriminate, stems not from some fallen angel who is outside of us, but from within us. We humans create the satan. The satan is the problem of mimetic desire which grasps.

This is not the end of the story though. Genesis 2–3 is connected to Gen 4 and the consequences of rivalry and violence in the story of Cain and Abel. It is only after the murder of Abel that Cain founds "civilization." This is the same process René Girard suggests occurs in founding murder myths: mediated desire, rivalry, violence, and the origin of human culture and religion. The Genesis text is not really different than ancient mythology in its structure. But, and this is a big but, it is very different in what it reveals in these connections. Myths occlude these connections; they have to, for they hide their victims. The revelatory component of the Genesis text is that the victim is no longer hidden; the victim has a voice ("your brother's blood cries out from the ground for vengeance").

And this revelation of the victim's voice makes all the difference. From Abel to Jesus to Stephen to Auschwitz and beyond, human history has, because of the biblical anthropology, been able to progressively hear the voice of the victim. This is what makes the Genesis text so powerful and so exceedingly relevant for today. All the evil in the world does not come from God, but from us. It has a structural form (culture) and it has a spiritual form (religion). Just as we humans are both *adama* (clay, soil, humus) and *ruach* (spirit, wind, breath) so also this reality we have created called civilization, human history, consists of both dimensions. There is a physical side to evil and there is a spiritual dimension to it as well.

The Genesis story has more to teach us about the problem of humanity than we realize. If we insist on a personal devil we will always be able to ultimately blame evil on God. When we accept that we humans are responsible for the horrors of our history, when we realize that the creation has been subjected to death so that we won't exist in this state forever, when we accept that Jesus's defeat of the satanic is the defeat of our grasping acquisitive ways, when we see him as the model for how to desire God alone, then, and only then, will we understand that we cannot but desire, and that Jesus has opened our eyes to desire the only object in the universe that lacks nothing, that fills everything, that truly satisfies, namely the One Jesus called Abba. God alone meets our deepest needs, yearnings, longings, and desires. And that, in a nutshell, is the point of the story of the man, the woman and the serpent in Genesis.

It is the Genesis text that clues us into our three questions: is the devil real, is the devil a person, and how is the devil overcome? Is evil real? It is hardly possible to listen or read the news without being acutely aware that something horrible has gone wrong with the human species and civilization.

As I sit here writing this there are rumblings of another potential global war. It may be possible that you are reading this on the other side of that.

Some might want to say that if God made us and we made evil, God should have known better and is ultimately responsible for it, a view akin to that of Isa 45. Or the question is framed, "How could a loving God create a world so full of evil?" This is the modern version of Voltaire's Enlightenment question juxtaposing divine goodness with divine omnipotence.

I have two things to say here. First, this question must be raised within the shadow of the cross, as all our questions must. Technically known as the problem of theodicy (how does one justify a god who seems not to be in control?), this question is often answered by an appeal to the satan. Blame it on the devil! What does the cross teach us about the satan?

You will recall the exercise I asked you to do by going to the passion narrative and looking for "God." Now do the same thing with regard to the satan. Is the satan present in the passion narrative? Certainly not as a figure, an evil malevolence. Does this mean that the satan is not present? The writers of the New Testament seemed to think so, especially Paul and the author of the Fourth Gospel. Where then is the satanic in the passion narrative?

Let us ask the question differently. Where is evil to be found in the passion narrative? Is it not in the reality of a grave injustice being done to an innocent person? Is it not also fact that this injustice is perpetuated under the category of law, that which is legal? And is it not further the case that this injustice appears to be motivated by the desire to maintain the national unity at the expense of another? Was it in fact "better that one man died than the nation perish" (John 11)?

Evil as injustice is Cain killing Abel. One must die in order for "a city to be built." Even so, another must die in order for the nation to thrive. We know this mechanism well. We practice it in our homes, our churches, our high school cliques. It is known as the act of scapegoating and it works best if you can get the scapegoated person to agree that you are right to be persecuting them, like Job's friends (who were condemned by God). When we are the ones in this position, it is easy to see that we are being railroaded. But, like the process of self-examination when it comes to our desires, so it is difficult to admit that we have participated in the scapegoating of others. We recognize the scapegoats of others, our own are hidden. Our victims "deserved" what they got, whereas the victims of our enemy were "unjustly treated." This is often how these kinds of events are reported in the mainstream media accelerating the frenzy.

This scapegoating process, this need for blood when things go wrong in our groups or cultures, has a very long history in our species. Over a very long period of time, we have encoded this mechanism into every part of our cultural life. It lies behind all of our judicial institutions, governments, banking and economics, political theory. But most of all, it can be found in our religions. Up until the modern period religion carried the message of sacrifice as life giving. Since then, as humanity has become more scientific and less superstitious, sacrifice has buried itself in our cultural institutions. Ask yourself this: Why are we always at war? Why can't there be peace on earth? Why do we kill in the name of god, or the name of the new god, the state? Why do we believe that god, or the gods, are interested in our wars and take our sides? Are we still stuck in the mythological paradigm of the ancients where gods took sides on earth? Yes, we are.

You see, this bloodthirsty mechanism is our salvation. As we developed as a species, we learned early on that indeed the way to handle our communal aggression was to, from time to time, find an outlet for that aggression, and we did. We learned to kill and eat one another. Cannibalism goes hand in hand with ancient sacrifice. To eat the dead was to consume their power, their mana, their magic. Ritual sacrifice of kings is a very old and common sacrifice. We learned to use violence homeopathically. It was better to take all of our aggression out onto a victim, or a set of victims, than to see the community implode and perish from internal conflicts run amok. A little violence, a little sacrifice brought a little, albeit temporal, salvation. Until the contagion of envy and hate arose again the next time.

We have already spoken about the move away from sacrifice that is occurring in the Bible. But it is only when we get to the cross of Jesus that we have exposed the breakage of the linkage between violence and divinity. It is the passion of Jesus and the telling of that passion that turned our human sacrificial mechanism of salvation into cosmic salvation for all. Remember, the passion narrative exhibits the structure of myth, the all-against-one story. But unlike myth, this victim is not guilty. On the contrary, *this* victim is totally innocent of the charges being brought against him. The Bible is subverting the way we humans tell the story about what makes us human. It is exposing the dirty little secret at the bottom of humanity's broken heart and mind. The gospel demystifies the lies told in myths. The gospel is the truth about persecutors and victims.

What about persecutors? This should be easy for all of you. Can you remember a time in your childhood where you joined the chorus of girls and boys who picked on a weaker member of your class? Perhaps you were in a clique in high school? Do you remember how you just joined in? Have you ever been in a church whose only reason for existence is being able to say, "we are not that"? Have you ever witnessed the process by which a small group of people grow into a loud chorus for the pastor to be removed? Have you ever at work joined the workers in your mutual disdain for your manager? Have you ever been in a family situation where you could easily (or so it seemed) blame someone on your family dysfunction?

Is it any wonder that the real question that converts us is not "are you a victim?" but "why do you persecute others?" Our original sin is not something we are born with; it is something we are born in to. It is human culture and its sacrificial ways. Our sinfulness lies in that we have been structured in deep psychological and spiritual ways by our culture. Culture is by its very nature sinful because culture is born from the practice of human sacrifice. There is no good human culture. There are just cultures on a scale of sacrificial to becoming less sacrificial; the only non-sacrificial culture that could ever exist prior to the advent of the reign of God is the community of the followers of Jesus.

Another way to talk about this is to examine Paul's use of the word *arkon*. First *arkon* is not a particularly religious word. It is mostly used in contexts of leadership or power. One could be the *arkon* of a synagogue, or one could be the *arkon* of demons. In 1 Corinthians, Paul, while speaking of the cross, mentions these *arkons*. In 2:6 Paul says the *arkontes* (plural of *arkon*) of this age will be nullified. I think there is a better translation though. I think Paul is aware of our human propensity to mix violence and the divine. Here in 1 Cor 2:6 Paul says that the *arkontes* of this age will be rendered powerless (and thus nullified), but it is most peculiar that the verb used shares a background with public lynching. Paul is in effect saying that these powers which engage us to participate in scapegoating will themselves be scapegoated from the market square by the many. This is the total renunciation of the connection between violence and the sacred. This is what the gospel is equipping us to do.

These *arkontes* had no clue that by bringing the true God into the very heart of their sacred solution they would render it inoperable and powerless. They had no idea that shedding the most precious blood in the universe, a blood which did not seek retaliation or vengeance, would result in the collapse of their deceitful lies that God either desired or wanted sacrifice. If they'd had a clue as to what was about to happen to them they would just have left Jesus alone to die of old age. These *arkontes* have a real physical dimension in religion, government, and just about all institutions, but they are far more than physical; like us, these *arkontes* are psychosocial, that is, they exist in relationship to us. The "spiritual" side of the *arkontes* is experienced as hell, judgment and suffering. Paul uses the term *arkon* for both physical and spiritual manifestations of the same reality: the false gods that we have erected in the temples of our mind and soul.

This is what makes idolatry so insidious. The idol binds us to itself so we come to believe that in this symbiotic relationship we would be deprived of ultimate reality should we ever leave our "god." That idol can be Zeus, or any god, including Christian representations of God. An idol can be a personality like presidential candidates, or an idol can be a cause like zeal or justice, which is to be served without compromise. Idols bind us to themselves and exert total control over not just what we think but how we think. I can guarantee that there will be many readers of this book who are afraid right now even as they read this. Will their idol burn them like toast for reading this little missive?

Our idols, our *arkontes*, are just that . . . ours! They are the structure of both our conscious worldviews and our subconscious intuition, thinking, and reactions. We all share a common *arkon* from the beginning: we are all susceptible to deception and death/killing. In a word, we, this thing we call humanity, the way we do human society or culture, are of the devil.

Recall our earlier discussion about the origins of evil and how a possible option was that of the two impulses or *yetzerim*. We might say that as we were evolving as a species we took a wrong turn, turning toward killing as salvation. Thus, all of our religion is tuned to killing and death as are our cultures. Our entire human existence is consumed with the category of death. After Cain opened the door to "sin," death followed ("Cain slew his brother Abel"), and then culture ("Cain went out and built a city").

If we conceive of evil, or the satan, as both a psychosocial projection of collective human non-conscious envy and rivalry, as well as the corresponding institutions that grow up around that to deal with it, we can see how it is that the Bible can say the "world" is in the grip of evil. The Bible speaks of this in terms of an original human couple and a talking snake, while we think of it in terms of an evolutionary process. Both amount to the same thing inasmuch as both ways of reading this text come up with similar anthropological insights about the human condition.

One of the more important aspects of reading the Bible from this perspective is that it answers so many unresolved questions about evil and suffering. Interestingly, even though James and Paul may disagree about the role of the Torah for the gentiles, they both have the same approach to "sinful" humanity. James, in a reflection on Gen 3–4, very neatly connects desire, rivalry, and ostracizing (scapegoating); here he speaks of the *yetzer* which falsely imitates and thus becomes "evil." Paul, in Rom 7, does the same thing, reflecting on the Adam (7:7–12) and Cain (7:13–20) narratives. Unlike James, Paul sees a culpability in the Torah as well; the law does not cure sin, it exacerbates it!

Our sinfulness is not something we are born with; it is something into which we are initiated from the moment of birth when we begin imitating the external world around us. Some fascinating research by Andrew Metzloff has shown that babies imitate facial expressions upon delivery.[1] We are human copy machines; this is how we learn, and it is also what we learn. This is because we are interdividual. You might say that we are programmed to imitate others around us, and we do. When we think our desires arise from with us, we can get envious of others who have what we want and so we begin the process of creating the enemy other, the one who has what I want but thwarts my plan to get it. Think here of Cain and Abel.

If evil does not come from without, if evil is not created by God and we humans are wholly responsible, this removes any superstition around evil. The world is not full of floating demons ready to take possession of unwitting souls; the human species, however, is full of unfulfilled desires creating resentment, rivalry, enemies, and conflict. We may experience such desires obsessively, passionately, indeed with zeal, and when we do they may well feel like we are possessed by another because in the sense that we have copied another's desire, it is true. We have given away our power and desired what the other desired. And like two-year-olds screaming in the grocery store, our souls scream and cry when our desires are not met. We foolishly think that if our desires were met, we would be fine. It turns out, however, that desire is (almost) infinite.

There is no need to blame the devil/the satan for all that is wrong in the world; we have but ourselves to blame. So, if like everything else we begin our reflections about evil from the perspective of the crucified, what is it we really see?

---

1. Garrels, *Mimesis and Science*, 55–74.

What the *arkontes* counted as their greatest success, the sacrifice of divine blood, became their greatest failure because the blood of Jesus failed to do what human blood had always done.

His blood spoke the truth. His blood spoke the truth about our human condition as persecutors and scapegoaters. His blood spoke the truth about the injustice of our legal systems and the tyranny of our governments. His blood spoke the revelatory truth that would forever disarm these "powers," his blood spoke a much better word than that of Abel. It was forgiveness, not vengeance that the dying Jesus sought. And this was not without some forethought by God.

John 17:16–24 indicates that Christian unity is found by accepting God's verdict that we are all persecutors and that we stand under the love shown to us in the cross of Christ. This is indicated in two ways, first in the use of *doxazo* (to glorify), which refers to the glory revealed in Jesus's suffering, and second in the phrase *katabole kosmou* (v. 24). It has two potential meanings which are not necessarily mutually exclusive. *Katabole kosmou* can mean from the "creation/foundation of the world" (= the created reality or nature), or from the "false creation of the world" (the foundation of human culture). The phrase occurs in Matt 13:35 (as a LXX quote from Ps 78:2), and again in Matt 25:34, Luke 11:50, John 17:24, Eph 1:4, Heb 4:3 and 9:26, 1 Pet 1:20, Rev 13:8 and 17:8. It is foreign only to the "genuine" Pauline letters. The translation of *katabole kosmou* will depend upon whether or not we see the *kosmou* as referring to the created order or to the "order" which we have created in victimage. In most cases, the *katabole kosmou* refers to the founding myth of Gen 3–4. There are two foundings, the founding or creation of God and the founding of human culture. The Johannine use of *kosmos* seems to us to indicate that it is the origins of the sacrificial mechanism that is in view, particularly when we consider the use of *doxazo*. Thus *katabole kosmou* in the Fourth Gospel should be understood as "the foundation of human culture."

As "the lamb slain before the foundation of the world," Jesus is the archetype of all victims. This is particularly true in Matt 25:34 and Luke 11:50 in the Synoptic tradition as well as Eph 1:4, 1 Pet 1:20, and the references in Revelation. There is no unity apart from the victim; the only question is whether that unity is unity against or with the victim. In the Johannine prayer of John 17, the unity that obtains between Jesus and the Father is the unity given to the believers, to those who have "believed Jesus '*logos*'" (message). The purpose of this unity is so that the *kosmos* might believe that the Father has sent the Son (17:21). It has been pointed out that on the road to Damascus, Jesus does not ask the apostle Paul, "Saul, Saul, why don't you believe in me?" but rather "Saul, Saul, why do you persecute me?" It is our persecutorial or retaliatory tendency (our "original sin") that is queried. Faith arises when we recognize our place as persecutors, as those who unjustly victimize, repent and take the side of the victim, breaking the false unity of the victimage mechanism. As long as those in Rome or Geneva or Washington, DC, insist on marginalizing others in the name of Jesus, they will not bear witness to the Lamb slain from the *katabole kosmou* but to the sacrificial myth, and so they will never experience the unity found in the Trinity.

The point of this is to indicate that the phrase *katabole kosmou* does not refer to some pre-history before Gen 1:1 but is a reference to the duplex of texts Gen 3 and 4. Some have erred in assuming that the work of Christ was "finished" prior to space, time, and history. In the Gospels there is a real threat, a very real possibility, that Jesus could go over to the dark side, to the use of retributive violence. Orthodox theology at this point makes the observation that "risk" is a theological category. Jesus could have blown it on any number of occasions by giving in to the test: use violence to achieve objectives.

"Foundation of the world" is taken by some to refer to creation, and election occurs before creation (*supralapsarianism*). But what if instead of translating *katabole kosmou* as "creation of the world" we translated it as "the founding of human culture"? There is a specific Greek noun for "creation" (*ktisis*). *Kosmos* as a term for the broken reality of our existence can be found in the Gospel of John. The *kosmos* is humanly constructed reality; it is how we live and think and believe and act. It is not perfect by any stretch of the imagination.

In this reading, "the lamb slain before the foundation of human culture" suggests implicit reference to Abel's murder in Gen 4. Has not Girard demonstrated that human culture originates in ritual sacrifice? Clear as bells he did.[2] Andrew McKenna puts it this way, "In the beginning was . . . the weapon."[3] Jesus articulated this line of thought also in Matt 23 by noting that the Jewish "canon" was bookended by murder.

---

2. Girard, *Things Hidden from the Foundation of the World*, 93–104.

3. Private conversation with the author.

In short, the problem of evil was planned for prior to the creation. Karl Barth refers to sin as the "impossible possibility."[4] It is as if one could say that when God set about creating there was a next to zero chance anything could go wrong, but if it did go wrong there was a contingency plan. That plan foresaw that it would be the problem of sacrifice ("lamb slain"), and this is also suggested by the author to the Hebrews. The author's critique of the older covenant is grounded in his exegesis of Ps 40 in chapter 10. Psalm 40 is most likely a critique of the Deuteronomic hermeneutic ("do good and you will be blessed, do evil and you will be cursed") found in the Hebrew Scriptures, which justifies sacrifice and often attributes violence to Yahweh. This Psalm is now found on the lips of the pre-incarnate Christ. The writer expressly connects the desire of God in the Psalm with the intention of Jesus in the incarnation. These personalist categories sharpen to cutting edge the critique of the sacrificial system. There is no distinction between the will of the Father and the will of the Son. This is crucial for those who contend for a propitiatory understanding of the atonement and also for those who would contend that Hebrews intends a sacrificial hermeneutic.

The sacrificial system is completely named: sacrifices, burnt offerings, and sin offerings. The citation of Ps 40 makes clear that God does not desire sacrifices, nor were they something that he ever wanted. In an editorial comment, the author also adds that God was not pleased with them. It would appear that the divine is in no way to be connected with the sacrificial system. The exegesis of Ps 40 in Heb 10:8–10 is one of the most critical exegeses in the New Testament and frequently overlooked. In the sense that the author of Hebrews discerns a crisis in the old sacrificial system, he exposes its weaknesses and limitations and transcends the old with the new.

Earlier I suggested that those texts that reveal the victimage mechanism and the relation of violence to the sacred are texts concerning which one can speak of revelatory significance. These texts have the power to deconstruct other texts and themselves. In this sense one can speak of an inner biblical hermeneutic. The author of Hebrews saw the distinction between revelation and religion when he contended that God neither wanted sacrifice nor was he pleased with it.

From the perspective of the crucified Christ, evil is a purely human phenomenon that exhibits two dimensions: the physical/institutional and the psychosocial or spiritual. Both sides of this are necessary if we are to

---

4. Barth, *Church Dogmatics*, 4/1:413–17.

properly understand how evil works in our lives and in our world. Walter Wink, in his magisterial trilogy on The Powers[5] underscores this both sides view of evil, that is, that evil is bound up with the way we structure our human relationships (government) and that it is also spiritual. What do I mean by this? If the devil is an idea, a construct that has taken many forms, and if we reject the divine origin of evil, then evil is something we humans have created. We can say that "we are the satan."

Can we say more? I think we can. If Girard is correct that our initial forays into the way we do this thing called "human" arises in violence done to innocent victims, and if we can now say that it is purely human projection that creates enemies of the other, we can also assert that the moorings of such a displacement are indeed spiritual in nature. We created gods and devils galore. The collective repeated acts of scapegoating, inevitably religious in nature (that is, we demonize our victims first; later we elevate them to gods), were projected onto that which is "outside of us." Early humans would have actually believed in gods and demons behind everything. For thousands, if not tens of thousands of years, humanity remained blind to its projections of divinity. This blindness becomes underscored when we recognize that our tales about our origins always included violence, but it was never *our* violence. We were not responsible; it was the gods or the devils that wrought calamities and disasters. From earliest times to the present, we humans would blame that which is outside of ourselves for bad things that happened to us. There is some truth to this. When we project our dark side, our anger, our hatred, our envy, we give it power over us; it becomes transcendent to us. We experience this malevolence outside of ourselves. We are unaware that this all arises from within us, because it comes from our non-consciousness. Over millennia of giving this darkness power, we have fallen prey to our imaginations and superstitions regarding just what darkness and evil are. We have replaced our own culpability with a horned and winged devil whom we can blame.

To claim that evil is human (or anthropological) in nature does not detract from its power. It is a Power, an *arkon*. It wreaks havoc in our world. Defeating this power or overcoming the devil is part of what Jesus does in his death and resurrection. This is accomplished in several different ways.

The first is to expose the lie of myth that the victim is truly guilty because they confess their guilt. The myth says they did so. Achan in Josh 7 is a good example of this. Israel is experiencing mimetic conflict in its

---

5. *Unmasking the Powers*, *Naming the Powers*, and *Engaging the Powers*.

military maneuvers and seeks to discern the problem. God figures the best solution is to guess, so a lottery is proposed. After a series of lots cast leaves only Achan, he then announces his guilt and is stoned by the entirety of the community. How easy it is to assume that "God" was somehow in collusion with this and accepted it. There is another story in the Gospels (albeit with a questionable textual history) about a woman caught in adultery (John 7:53—8:11). This woman was also perceived as the cause of problems in a certain community and was brought to be stoned. Notice what Jesus does and doesn't do.

He does not enter into the question of the woman's guilt or innocence. He does not seek to discern whether the charges were valid or not. He does not take her side. He does not stand in some kind of liberal solidarity with her and proclaim her innocence. Rather he suggests that stoning would be acceptable if, and only if, anyone who threw a stone were in a state of purity, that is, without sin. The eldest among the mob leave first, nobody throws the first stone, and Jesus's admonishment to the woman is to eliminate the behavior that brought her to such a place. In other words, Jesus's breaks the mob fiction that seeks differentiation (we are not sinners like this woman) by trapping the mob to acknowledge they are no different than the woman. The human community cannot discern between good and evil; it calls good that which is evil and evil that which is good. This is because our divinity is Janus-faced, and we never know when we are on God's good side and when we are on God's naughty list. So religion comes in and makes up ways we can know this, and furthermore, in order to safeguard that knowledge, it engages in all manner of sacrifice to blind us to our own self-inflicted horror. Recall our discussion of this in the first chapter when we identified the five pillars of Protestant Orthodoxy:

- The inerrancy or infallibility of the Protestant Bible
- The penal substitutionary atonement
- Eternal conscious torment (Hell)
- A theology of glory
- Sacrificial thinking

I would add to this list the justification of violence.

The early Jewish priest(s) that composed Gen 2–11 completely demystified the devil. You might ask, "what about when Jesus says to his interlocutors in John 8, 'You are of your father, the devil, who was a liar and a murderer from the beginning'"? Did not Jesus equate the snake with the devil? That is just half the truth. Liar refers to Gen 3, but the liar becomes the murderer, and the murderer is a human being, Cain. Shall we assume that Cain was possessed by the devil? No, for the text tells us it was "sin" crouching at the door, not the "devil."

The mystery of sin is exposed. It is human self-deception that creates a crisis that ends in death. Jesus's passion exposes this lie by assuming the same all-against-one structure of myth; it inverts it so that he becomes the-one-for-all, reminiscent of what Dietrich Bonhoeffer said when he stated "Jesus Christ, the human for other humans."[6]

A second way Jesus overcomes the satan in the passion narrative is to counter the prosecutorial ways of the enemy with forgiveness, freely offered, in the name of his Father. If the satanic is the prosecuting principle, its opposite would be a defender, and this is just what we have in the gospel. The Fourth Gospel calls the Holy Spirit our Defender (*paraclete*). We have a divine counterpart to our adversary. Where the adversary lies, the Holy Spirit leads us to knowledge of Jesus as the truth. Where the adversary accuses, the Holy Spirit defends and where the adversary kills, the Holy Spirit brings life. It would take us too far afield, but I would note that the Fourth Gospel's view of the Spirit is intimately bound up with a theology of the cross. As the writer says in his first letter, "Jesus came . . . by spirit, water and blood," surely a reference to the stabbing of the spear into Jesus side just after he "pneumaed" his last *pneuma* (spirit/breath).

A third way Jesus overcomes these false *arkontes* in his dying was to announce to one of the terrorists hanging with him that this very day they would meet in "paradise." Death does not have the last word; it is just a penultimate word. The last word, the final word that is spoken is life, life-giving, peace, a word of an utterly new creation. The words of Jesus to the terrorist hanging with him is a testament to Jesus's faith in the Father to let him live on, and so Jesus trusted that the Father would raise him from the dead, which happened on that first Easter Sunday.

The powers that be believe that their authority extends through all time and beyond the grave. They believe that the historical judgments that are formed about the innocence or guilt of victims will always hold true. They thought that killing the Truth-teller would solidify their community and bring peace from the chaos which erupted from time to time in Second Temple Jewish culture. They were wrong. Because of the resurrection of

---

6. *Letters and Papers from Prison*, 8:501.

Jesus, their lies were exposed and continue to be exposed anywhere his passion story is read.

It is important to note that victims are not necessarily innocent, but they are like lightning rods. Once a victim is selected by the crowd (through lottery, finger pointing, or judicial arraignment) guilt must be attributed. In our own time we see this, especially where governments seek to silence their critics by attributing to them the worst possible crimes, these days usually some sort of pedophilia, a most heinous crime. Oedipus, Job, the suffering servant, celebrities, politicians, anyone involved in the Power System becomes fair game when it comes to functioning as a scapegoat.

It is the message of the gospel that has, for the past two thousand years, been deconstructing our worldviews, our ideas, and ideologies, our theologies and philosophies. The early church did their best to frame the sickness of human culture in the language that they knew: that of the spiritual realm of either the gods or of the dark side. They believed in actual demonic spirits floating in the air waiting to just jump in and inhabit people. Certain Pharisees in Jesus's day avoided shadows because they believed demons dwelt in dark spaces. This would be commonplace up until the seventeenth century and the Enlightenment.

We now no longer speak of demonic possession but of neurological or psychological disorders. We have learned to deal with "the possessed" of our own time by medicating them. Like the Gerasene demoniac, who functioned as the community's scapegoat, we "subdue/medicate" our victims, keep them away from ourselves, and confine them to locked rooms. What is it that "the possessed" suffer from that makes them vulnerable targets? I have two observations. Long ago Gregory Bateson noticed a correlation between schizophrenia and double binds.[7] Double binds occur when two conflicting commands are given. A humorous example I use comes from the late comedic writer Erma Bombeck. She imagines a child at a dinner table whose mother says, "Don't talk to me with your mouth full, answer me!" This is a classic double bind. One's mouth is full, and one is not allowed to talk but is being commanded to talk thus violating the other "law." Many of us have experienced this kind of reality. It is the way of the Janus-faced god.

The death of Jesus sets us free from double binds like, "God loves you unconditionally but if you don't believe you will burn in hell forever." The couple created their own double bind in the garden. Notice how they added to the prohibition, and even after that when the woman ate the fruit nothing

---

7. Bateson, *Steps to an Ecology of the Mind*.

happened. No judgment, no sin, no death. It takes two to tango and it takes two to sin. Sin is a relational, not a moral category. Sin is "the destructive way we handle our pain" (Rev. Denny Moon).[8] Jesus's death sets us free by announcing that death does not have the last word because neither sin nor the prosecuting angel have the last word.

Second, in an essay done some years ago by Stephen Morris using the work of criminologist Lonnie Athens, the link between imitation and violence is made clear by Athens. Athens studied criminals, the worst violent offenders. He sought to understand their decision-making process and compared it to those who made conscious nonviolent decisions. He observed:

> I think that violent criminals are made through a brutalization process, usually at a young age, during which they make choices but at certain points they have greater leeway to make choices than other parts. And it starts with the process of being brutalized. And they don't make the choice to be brutalized. Their brutalizers make the choices for them. They're the subject of violent subjugation. They're subject to personal horrification. Soon mentors come along to violently coach them. Then in the second stage, if they get there, they get in a defiant stage, they become belligerent. And as a result of reliving their brutalization they have an epiphany that the only way they can stop their brutalization is to become violent themselves. And then they enter into a violent performance stage where they test their resolve. People become fearful in their presence and they come to embrace that, having experienced malevolency, deciding to enjoy their violent notoriety. They soon delight in social trepidation. And then they decide at this point that for the slightest provocation to attack people with the serious intention of killing them or gravely injuring them. But here's the irony. When they began the process, they were just a hapless victim of brutalization, but at the end they become the ruthless aggressor who they earlier had despised. And so, this is the context in which the decisions are made.[9]

This is so similar to the insights of the priestly writer of Genesis as well as James and Paul, namely that we humans are fragile, moldable, and above all conformists. We will follow the herd in order to avoid being singled out; those who are different, those who are not "normal," are easily singled

---

8. Private conversation with author.
9. Morris, "Nature of Mimetic Desire," 2.

out and thus easy marks for becoming a potential scapegoat. Furthermore, Morris notes that within all of us is a "phantom community."[10] We might note that this has been called many things, from our collective unconscious to our collective soul, to cosmic consciousness or as I put it, "the radio dial in our heads." This "phantom community" is a collection of all the voices we have heard in our lives, some telling us this, some telling us that, often leaving us in confusion and despair as to what should be done.

Here is Stephen Morris:

> The "generalized other" is not the voice of a general social normativity, but of a "phantom community." The "phantom community" is the "other" we address when we speak to ourselves. It is the collective voice of all the people who have been significant to us in some way. It is part of the unconscious but emerges in times of profound crisis. His [Athens] insight from extensive interviews with violent offenders is that they have different phantom communities from the rest of us, which is why the advice they receive is so radically different. Their phantom communities interpret the attitudes and behavior of their victims as fearful, angering, or hateful, and recommend violence in response. But again, the phantom community does not only influence the ultraviolent: it is a universal phenomenon.[11]

When voices conflict at a deep structural level in a person the overwhelming anxiety and fear they experience can morph into self-inflicted pain (cutting, masochism, suicide, etc.). Such folks live with a dark cloud over their heads. Everything is wrong with the world and their life is barely worth living. Behind most of these conflicts lies some sort of double bind. I have known more than a few persons who experienced a nervous breakdown because while they believed "God" loved them, they were so fearful of an eternity in hell it broke their minds.

Jesus's death brings an end to all of this. All of our worldviews are crucified at Calvary. All of our theologies and philosophies, all of our common so-called wisdom, all of the nonsense we have heard, absorbed and lived our lives by is terminated. All law is terminated ("Christ is the end of Torah," Rom 10). Because all law is crucified, so are all the powers behind any law (Col 2:13–15). Inasmuch as all law is done away with there is no

---

10. Morris, "Nature of Mimetic Desire," 4.
11. Morris, "Nature of Mimetic Desire," 4.

room left for any prosecutor, so the satan as an idea and as a real *arkon* is also crucified and dies.

The death of Jesus nullifies all cosmic powers that we have created and to which we have become subservient. These cosmic powers are very real; I think of them as our collective nonconscious AI. We created them through the homeopathic use of violence; we sustain them with this same curative formula. However, after two thousand years, we can see with faces unveiled that a little violence does not put an end to greater violence. We have become aware of all of the horrid things we humans have done in exploiting others, exterminating others, colonizing others, all in order to maintain our own society or culture or group or family.

In the long run, it is impossible for me to understand the category of the devil as a "person" in the way the majority define "person." Evil is not autonomous, and there is much wisdom in saying evil is the absence of something, be it light or love. Evil has no ontology, it does not exist in and of itself, it exists only in relation to that which is not. Karl Barth used the term "Das Nichtige" which means something like "that which is not" with reference to the dark side.[12]

There is a way to understand the apostolic witness to the death of Jesus that has to do with a conquering of the *arkontes*, which does not depend on the Enoch myth or medieval superstition or Hollywood. By taking a purely anthropological approach we can verify the reality of the satanic in our world, its horrors and ill effects, and at the same time we can see that evil is unmasked in the cross of Christ.

Where the satanic impulse would single out the One Jesus Christ, and the human species has followed this gesture ever since, the resurrection of Jesus from the grave and his subsequent ascension to the Father puts an end to all of our communal madness. We can move from being the Pharisees who mocked Jesus or the soldiers of the state who crucified him to becoming nonviolent, nonretaliatory witnesses like the women and the beloved disciple.

This is not all that can be said of the cross of Jesus for we too are crucified, nevertheless we live (so says Paul in Gal 2:20). We too die on Calvary. There we are forgiven and in his death we die. But we also live in his death because he gives us an example to follow. He calls us to be forgiving as well and non-retaliatory. Did he not invite us to carry our cross every day? This

---

12. Barth, *Church Dogmatics*, 3/3:289–368.

is not about generic suffering; it has specifically to do with our behavior toward those who hurt us.

The good news of the gospel is that God is light, and the Light of the Father has penetrated the entire cosmos of human understanding, intuition, awareness, and consciousness. The darkness is fading away. Yes, this is difficult because it forces us to see ourselves as we really are: a wicked cannibalistic species. We hate being shown that our unmet desires are really just imitation. We despise being shown that our envy and greed are not virtues. We revolt at being shown that we are just like everyone else. We rail as our cultures break down, but break down they must because they are built on the sand of blood and violence. When we do away with violence and violating the other then we shall know peace.

# 5

# Reframing Christian Doctrine

We have come a long way in our understanding of what makes the gospel truly good news. We have seen that understanding the Bible from an anthropological perspective is not a contradiction of viewing the Bible from a theological point of view. In this chapter I would like to show you how I see the relation between a mimetic anthropological perspective and that of the great doctrines of Christian theology.

Twenty years ago, I produced a chart. On the left-hand side of the page, I placed all of the elements of the mimetic theory of René Girard. Then on the right side of the page I placed the great dogmas and doctrines of Christianity. As I unfolded this it became clear to me that our trust in the great thoughts of Christendom could be substantiated. Could one come up with a doctrine of the Trinity that was actually an exodus from the old gods? Could one show how the Trinity and the cross were intimately related? Could one further show how the Trinity, the cross, and the church/Christian life were related? This was my goal.

As these past two decades have unfolded and we have seen new and increasingly aggressive streams of Conservative/Evangelical Christianity and modern Christian liberalism move farther and farther from either understanding, or embracing (or both), and most certainly from living as if these great doctrines truly matter, and as I have matured in my own life and understanding, this has taken on an urgency for me. What are we leaving for the next generation to grab onto? How can those of us, like myself, who have dedicated lifetimes now to the hard work of true theological scholarship for the sake of discovering the gospel's real "GOOD NEWS" pass something of value on to those who come after us? How might we spare them so much of the wrong-headed/religion-driven/false narrative/life-sucking understanding of the Bible and the gospel that we, in our generation (and the ones before), have had to endure? How might we show them a purified path to the Father? I believe we sit on the precipice of rare opportunity as the revelations of the past two centuries usher in a new gospel-oriented era. It is my hope that this book and its sequel will contribute to the fruitful recovery and forward momentum of the church of the next generation.

Back to the chart. I will go through this point by point and explain my reasoning. I took as my cue the critical role the cross plays in discerning human from divine wisdom in 1 Cor 1–2. We know there is a division, the question is, "how do we frame the question?" What does "divine culture" look like? Oddly enough, we Christians have known all along. We just failed to do two things: we failed to demystify the devil, and we failed to connect the dots between the Trinity and the cross. When we do these two things we can see the truth about ourselves and the truth about God. And the truth will set us free.

The best way to understand this chart is to become familiar with the components of the mimetic anthropology, as depicted on the left side of the chart; desire, which is imitated and leads to rivalry where persons are indistinguishable from the other, which in turn leads to the need for an outlet, thus precipitating the all-against-one mechanism of scapegoating. The result of this is human religion and culture.

The right side shows us the truth of what we have distorted and how the revelation of the true and living God corresponds in some detail to the way we humans do religion (and culture). The right side begins with the Trinity and moves through the trinitarian revelation in Jesus to the church and the new life brought by the Holy Spirit who raised Jesus from the dead. It concludes with the true foundational pillars of the reign of God.

The entire point of this little book is to show how intimately theology and human relations are intertwined, or how followers of Jesus are transformed in not only what and how they think, but also in how they live in relation to others, the creation and themselves. There is no guesswork about what is right or what is wrong where God reigns, for there is no external law. The world needs its laws; there is only the law or obligation to love within the Christian community. Does this mean anarchy reigns there? Not at all.

| **God's No!** | **(I Cor 1:19-22)** | **God's Yes!** |
|---|---|---|
| **Negative Mimesis** | | **Positive Mimesis** |
| **'Human Culture'** | | **'Divine Culture** |

1. *Desire* (James 1:13, 4:1ff)  *Desire*
   -triangular nature of                    -trinitarian nature of; *perichoresis*

   -imitated (I-Thou-I)                    -God as Subject (I-Thou) Jn 5:16-30

   -object oriented                          -Desiring God's desire; God's will


2. *Rivalry ------ Model/Obstacle*      *Self-Giving* (Non-Rivalrous)
   -volatile nature of (Gen 2-4)         -*humilitas* Phil 2:5-11 hymn on Gen 2-3

   -escalation of imitated actions     -surrender/trust (pistis Xristou)

   -Other oriented (subject as enemy)   -Subject oriented (subject beloved)


3. *Undifferentiation* (Romans 1:17-32)    *Undifferentiated Differentiation*
                                                                          (God as Trinity)

[----the point of no return-----]

(All imitate all; need for differentiation)    Son imitates Father    Father Glorifies Son

                                (cross)          (resurrection)

|              | Hebrews 12:24 | (priest)      |          (king)       |

Violence                    Love

Revenge                    Forgiveness

| Logos of Heraclites | Logos of the Fourth Gospel |
|---|---|
| The Cover-Up | The Truth |

----- Adam (Romans 5:12-21) Christ -----

Christus Victor (Col 1:15-20) Exemplary Model

| *Scapegoat* (differentiated victim) | *Spirit in One = Body of Christ* |
|---|---|
| -all against one | (ascension) one for all Col 3:1-4 |
| -the 'lie' of individuality | (prophet) truth of oneness/interdividual |
| -*j'accuse'* The Satan | The Paraclete ((*pro nobis*) Jn 16:12-15 |
| -*meconnaisance* | *anamnesis* (memory & hope) |
| -Phantom Community | Voice of the Good Shepherd |
| -(religious) addiction (Rom 7) | Brain transformation (mirror neurons) |

| *Sacralization* | *Resurrection as Vindication* |
|---|---|
| -victim agent of chaos/order | -vindicated victim agent of new order |
| -victim as binary symbol | -victim (Jesus) as unitary symbol |
| -origins of dualism (Zoroaster, Plato) | -demise of dualism (Barth, Derrida) |

*Job* (Exile – Return) 2*ⁿᵈ Isaiah*

| *Pillars of Culture* | | *Prophetic Critique of Culture* |
|---|---|---|
| 1. Prohibition (Law) | | 1. New Covenant (Jer 31.31ff) |
| 2. Ritual (Religion) | | 2. Self-Giving as Eucharist |
| -'*do ut des; lex talionis* | | -*phero/anaphero* and cognates |
| 3. Myth (Discourse, Literature) | | 3. Gospel (the story of Jesus) |
| theology of glory | [Luther] | theology of the cross |
| hermeneutics from above | [Bonhoeffer] | hermeneutics from below |

When the church today claims that it is a loving, inclusive community it lies, for behind every church that claims this exists hidden scapegoats. What started out as a quest for freedom morphed into the desperate need for differentiation (and attention), thus bringing about the greatest crisis since the Reformation: the sexual revolution of the 1960s brought us the multi-gendered revolution of the twenty-first century and the dissolution of Christianity. Just look at the number of mainline churches that were torn down the middle on sex/gender issues.

If the church had truly been the church these never would have become issues. Our vision is to be something not just greater or better. Our vision is to be of a different order altogether. We seek to show that Christian dogma, rightly understood, is non-sacrificial in its orientation. We have had to examine where the church bought into presuppositions that were alien to the gospel and to challenge those assumptions. I think it is fair to say that Protestant Orthodoxy and those theologies that developed out of it, including Evangelicalism and Fundamentalism is a dead end. Why? That tradition has reified its doctrine, it has made belief in doctrinal positions the keystone to faith. It has turned trust (*pistis*) into an intellectual operation. And at every turn, whether it is a doctrine of election or atonement or eschatology or the church, there are in and out groups. The gospel which is anti-sacrificial is completely occluded in the Protestant tradition.

Now a word about liberal Protestant Christianity in America today. When one examines the emphases of this tradition it seems clear to me that inclusivity, justice, and tolerance seem to be the key watchwords. One can certainly find in the ministry of Jesus these emphases, but they are totally reframed. Jesus's emphases were not today's modern liberal emphases.

A hundred years ago Albert Schweitzer wrote his book on the first quest of the historical Jesus and concluded Jesus was a frustrated social prophet who sought to change human history and, having failed to secure the social revolution he sought, ended up being crucified and now spins on the wheel of history for all to see. Today's modern liberals have pretty much the same picture. This is primarily due to the fact that liberal Christianity has no resurrection; for them the stories of the resurrection of Jesus are legends created by the early church. Jesus was a great social prophet, not the unique Son of the Father. I realize this comes as a surprise to some, but it is true.

Liberal Christianity will fail for the same reasons Schweitzer saw Jesus failing. However, I would rather follow a liberal failing Jesus than the Jesus of Protestant Orthodoxy. I find the moralistic Jesus to be a false historical picture of the rabbi from Nazareth. Liberals rightly see Jesus proclaiming a message of a different order, however, it is the case that in this quest they have become as religious, i.e., sacrificial, as the Conservative Christians.

America is at the beginning of its religious civil war. Two visions of America as a "Christian" nation are on offer, and both believe they have the right reading of the Bible to justify their positions. The real issue for me is that both sides would see their vision brought to fruition by the government. This would automatically require that form of Christianity to be sacrificial, for American culture is replete with victims and scapegoats. Whether conservative or liberal, Christianity was never meant to become part of the world order. That it became such and has remained so for eighteen hundred years does not invalidate this. Christians too easily equate church and society, theology and social questions, spirituality and superstition. The gospel message is of such a different order. It is not about apples and oranges. The gospel paradigm shift is so profound it can hardly be compared to anything we know. Jesus had to resort to parables, riddles (*mashalim*), and questions just to get his hearers to think outside their boxes. Jesus's teaching on the reign of God is focused on how God reigns, and God does not reign like governments and religious communities do.

Where God reigns there is love for all, peace among all, and joy in all. When a community only loves those inside its doors or those who toe their party line, they are not loving with the love of God. When a community engages in strife, one-uppance, envy, gossip, name calling and slander, its peace is false. And when a community celebrates victory over another community its joy is a lie because that joy has come at the expense of another.

Within the body of Christ we may hold to many different opinions about many different things. However, where Christian reading of the Bible and Christian doctrine end up with a dualism, creating in and out groups, there is a significant problem. Readings that justify sacrificial thinking are contrary to a gospel interpretation of Scripture. Instead of recognizing that gospel demystifies myth, sacrificial interpreters of the Bible distort and invert the gospel so that it becomes just another in a long line of religious practices. Little wonder that the seventeenth century Enlightenment thinkers could look back on the history of Christianity with the Thirty Year's War (1618–48) in the rear-view mirror and declare that there was something wrong with this God.

Voltaire and others saw that the claims of Christianity were not just false, but detrimental to human society. The Calvinists of that time saw things differently; they would create the kingdom of God on earth, through war, colonization, and slavery. Modern thinkers clearly saw the problems with sacrificial Christianity, even if they could not put their finger precisely on this as we are able to today. In his book *Age of Anger*, Pankaj Mishra clearly demonstrates that even the Enlightenment got caught up in the Christian/religious ways of sacrificial thinking. Voltaire and Rosseau would justify the use of force/violence to advance the aims of the Enlightenment.

Every single political experiment done either in the name of God, or in the name of being anti-God, has ended in bloodshed. The world is awash in sacrificial logic, and it is this sacrificial thinking that the gospel has come to set us free from so that we can become healthy beings-in-relation, and thus live into the life of the Trinity.

As I mentioned earlier, it is easy to see someone else's scapegoats. It is damn near impossible to see one's own. The question I raise at this time is this: is it the purpose of the gospel to correct, rehabilitate, or destroy human culture? I am reasonably certain most of you will opt for one of the first two choices, that the purpose of the gospel is to make the world a better place to live. If this choice is made it requires that one knows what is wrong with the world, and herein lies our crisis.

The diagnoses of modern Christian liberalism and that of Conservative/Evangelical Christianity are entirely different. The liberal looks across society and sees injustice, the conservative sees immorality. The conservative move toward creating a theocracy in America is only different in kind but not in type to the liberal Christian ideal of forcing social change through awareness, solidarity, protests, etc. Both find their final solution in the American political process. For the Left, this is part of Dr. Martin Luther King Jr.'s legacy, for the right it is that of Puritanism. Both sides seek to become the majority and both sides are as mimetically entangled as they have ever been. Both sides claim the moral high ground and both sides are in a pitched feverish battle "for the soul of America."

God the Father, revealed in Jesus Christ by the Spirit, is not to be found in this battle. This is not a battle between good and evil, light and darkness. It is a battle for who will retain the high priestly right to control the blood sacrificial mechanism. No matter which side "wins," everybody loses because today's battle is just another in a hundred thousand string of variants on Cain and Abel. The "truth" cannot be found in either form of American Protestant Christianity. Both sides justify violence, and oddly enough, in a great misinterpretation of the text(s), both sides appeal to Jesus's alleged violence and "protest" in the temple.

And so it is that generation after generation we continue to make Jesus into our own sacrificial image. Clergy do it, scholars do it. Remember, anti-Christs, false portraits of Jesus, have been around since the first century. At the end of his letter, the writer says, "Children, keep yourself from idols" (1 John 5:20). We have several reasons to think that he is here referring to false understandings of Jesus, particularly his death. We Christians have in our DNA a need to create a sacrificial Jesus, and thus a sacrificial god, because we cannot face the truth that the gospel reveals about ourselves: that we, not God, are vampiric, bloodthirsty, vengeful, and split in ourselves.

And yet, through all of the occlusion, the whitewashing, the twisting of the gospel, the Christian tradition has managed to give us the great dogmas that challenged Christianity itself again and again and again throughout the ages. The fourth-century church bequeathed to us a Creed, the only universal creed in Christianity. The Nicene Creed is both beautiful and lacking. It is beautiful inasmuch as it addressed their contemporary theological issues; it is lacking however, in failing to mention Jesus's mission and message. I get that that wasn't their concern, but it is our concern today.

If the Trinity means anything it means that God is like Jesus. Now I know that all the language surrounding *homoousias* (of the same substance) sought to show that Jesus is divine, but today we really need to ask a different question. Our question is not whether Jesus is like God, as though we know what a god is supposed to be (usually a collection of nouns, adverbs, and participles). Since the Shoah (the Holocaust), god concepts have died a thousand deaths, especially concepts of God that are little more than the attribution to God of human virtues exponentially multiplied (we know some things, God is omniscient, we have a presence, God is omnipresent, etc.). This kind of a god died not just in the years 1942–45, but also in 33 CE, when a healer from Galilee was crucified in a public execution.

Our question today, knowing what we know about Jesus, has been transformed. We are wondering if God is like Jesus, and, if God is like Jesus, then that means the transformation of all our theological thinking. This is why I think it essential to still retain the formula of the Nicene Creed, but also find that we can rethink it in terms more conducive to our changed philosophical mindset. I believe that Jesus redefined and continues to redefine our theology. That is, his vision of the character of God, whom he called Abba, is meant to bring about real transformation intellectually, socially, psychologically, and spiritually. Imagine what the world would be like if God was like Jesus. Imagine what power sermons would have if Jesus was truly proclaimed as Lord, and not just in some glib way but as the archetype of all that is real and true. Imagine what the Body of Christ would look like if it looked like Jesus.

That is what I do all day long. I imagine a world where Jesus is all in all and that is why I still have hope for the Christian faith, for theology, and for the gospel as the Spirit works in our world.

Now back to our chart.

The left-hand side of the page frames a biblical anthropology. It begins with Gen 2–11 for a reason. The problem with beginning with Gen 1:26 KJV, "Let us make man in our image, after our likeness," is that we think we can actually understand that text as though we're not in Gen 3 as a species. Once we engaged in negative mimesis, once we were expelled from the garden, all theology from that point on is idolatry. All theology. All thinking about God.

The "Adam" so to speak, the mythic Adam and Eve figures, they're not able to think, "Hey, let's talk about what the real image of God is." They don't know it. All they know is this broken image thing that they've got going. That's all they know. And that's all we've ever known until this revelatory process enters in.

But when you try, as many do, taking your definition of being made in the image and likeness of God from the creation story, you're assuming that there's nothing wrong with your head. Like nothing went down in Gen 3. That's what you're assuming. You're assuming you can bypass Gen 3 and get right to Gen 1 about what it means to be made in the image and likeness of God. So, you're reasonable—God is reasonable. You're rational—God is rational. You're linguistic—God is linguistic. You're emotional—God has emotions, but God has "controlled" emotions. Whatever, whatever. You just project yourself out onto God, that's all you're doing.

No. This is to place the cart before the horse. We've done theology bent ever since Gen 3, friends. We can't get this God image and likeness thing right, and that's why he sent Jesus in the flesh. The Word made flesh. Jesus is the icon, the image, and the likeness of God. Alone. Period. Not some original Adam and Eve figures in a garden, in a mythic story. No, the image and likeness of God is found in the historical Jesus of Nazareth, and the church's proclamation of him. That's where the image and likeness of God is found. Do you see this? There's no other place you can look for the character of the Creator than Jesus of Nazareth. That's the assertion of the New Testament—if you want to know the character of the Creator then you look at Jesus. End of story. That's it. Jesus alone has been vindicated by being raised from the dead. He has been vindicated by alone being seated at the right hand of the Father. That alone is the image and likeness of God. Him alone.

And that's why it's important that you recognize, as you think through his teachings and live them out, as you seek to discern his presence through your life and the various phases you go through, that Jesus alone interprets God. That's the conclusion to the prologue of the Gospel of John, one of the greatest texts in the world: Jesus exegetes the Father (John 1:1–18).

The first creation story is an eschatology, it tells us where everything is going. It gives us hope in spite of what is to follow. Genesis 2–11 is the realistic story about how we got where we are. Scripture begins with salvation, light shining in darkness, and order coming out of disorder. As I have noted in several places, what makes the first creation story unique is that unlike other ancient origin stories, the first creation story contains no violence, no blood. It is a completely non-sacrificial creation. But we are not the androgynous couple in the text living in peace and harmony. We come to this business of discerning of the image of God from a place of broken thinking. Our theology, like that of the couple in Gen 3, begins in fear. We too have lived with a Janus-faced deity within Christianity for two thousand years. But we have seen now how the gospel exposes this, and how, because of the revelation of the Trinity in the crucified Jesus, we are free to trust the gospel—for it is truly astonishing good news.

A mimetic anthropology is not the only way one might construct a view of the human being, but it is a very realistic one. It considers everything from the intrapersonal (desire) to the social (rivalry), to religion (scapegoating ritual) and human culture. In other places I have given references to the science that continues to illumine the mimetic anthropology (*The Jesus Driven Life*, *Mimetic Theory and Biblical Interpretation*). And here I would note that when Girard set about his journey of unveiling the mimetic theory in relation to sacrifice and religion, he did the unthinkable as a scientist: he turned to the Bible. And it was the insight of Holy Scripture that opened Girard's eyes to the relation of the gospel to religion. In other words, and I hope to have shown this to some degree, the mimetic anthropology is one derived from science and Scripture.

Ok, so far so good, but what of theology? Isn't theology just human guesswork?

One could say that such is the case given the fact we have literally, and I mean literally, tens of thousands of interpretations of the Bible over the centuries. How can any claim be made that theology is a science? To suggest that theology is a science just means that the same rational processes we use in the human and physical sciences will also be applied to theology. Note I said "rational processes" for there is a fair amount of theological writing that is purely speculative.

The thing is that "God" is not a category that can be known. It can be imagined (and often is), it can be that God is anything—to the infinite degree. God is a superlative of our own projections. Some of the most intelligent atheists have seen this including Feuerbach, Nietzsche, Marx, and Freud. God to the thousandth power is still human projection. When we try to apply religious categories to "God" we end up with either the atheist rejection of revelation or the cultish superstition of lay Christianity. We simply are not capable of understanding ourselves in relation to divinity, because the divinity we seek to relate to is ourselves, our very Janus-faced Gen 3 selves.

But we would not even know any of this were it not for the light of the goodness of the gospel which shines in the face of Jesus Christ. We would have no idea of our tendencies to deceive, mislead, and covet. We would not become aware that we are bloodthirsty, ladder climbing, favor-seeking broken mirrors. Were it not for God's willingness to come into the very heart of that which we humans created, religion/theology, we would not have a clue. It is hardly possible to conceive of the love it took to enter into the most extreme madness of our civilizational hell. That which was loved so very much would ignore, misunderstand, betray, deny, and execute the Lover.

If we had done this to any of the gods of our phantasmagoric religions, that god would have come back pissed and out for justice! Not so the God of the gospel, the Father of Jesus, the Maker of all that is. Into the lost abyss of total rejection our God goes, willingly, and forgiving all those who trespass against him(her). The God of the gospel does not enter into rivalry with the creature. The God of the gospel humbles God's self to take the form of a servant . . . and die a criminal's death (Phil 2:5–11). Is this God crazy? Has this God lost God's mind? Gods just don't behave this way. Not for nothing, but the earliest graffiti about Christianity is from the late second century, showing an ass's head and a human body on a Roman cross with the words "Alexamenos worships his god."

How does pure Love and Light come into this world? By becoming human, it became possible for light and love to be brought to our brutish species. This is not metaphysical mumbo jumbo but actual, concrete salvation that begins with us humans learning to imitate real divinity as seen in the life and teaching of Jesus of Nazareth. The gospel does not present us with a set of laws to obey; it gives us a person to willingly imitate. How do we do this? We learn to suffer. And in suffering we trust that light will prevail over darkness even, and often in spite of what we think or know. We learn to suffer and instead of retaliating we forgive. We learn to suffer and instead of demanding justice we freely give ourselves away. This path of the cross is the Christian path. This is not some sado-masochistic path. One does not seek to suffer, in fact, one should try to avoid suffering. But when it comes, and it will come, how we undergo our suffering is what sets us apart from the world.

We learn how to be divine not by knowing good and evil (which we seem to have fucked up in a grand manner), but by practicing humility in relation to others just as God has done with us in Jesus. What does this have to do with theology being a science?

Karl Barth began his magisterial *Church Dogmatics* with a discussion of theology as a science.[1] Thomas Torrance sought to show how the "way of knowing"[2] in Einstein and Athanasius was the same. Alister McGrath has written the brilliant series on *The Science of God*. In each case, the authors argue that one cannot come to "Christian theology" from the outside, objectively. Rather, authentic Christian theology begins with the process of trust: trust that God is who God says they are in Jesus Christ. The trustworthiness of the message and the messenger is the point of the gospel message. This makes theology a very personal matter, for each theological thinker (and that is all of us) must trust that the message is trustworthy. And how does one do this? By undergoing the same process Jesus did. But whereas he was uniquely discipled by the Father, we are all discipled by him. We come to know the Father as we follow Jesus.

The Anabaptist Hans Denck said, "No one can truly know Christ unless he follows him in life." Or, another way is to say that to know Christ is to follow him, and to follow him is to know him. There is no purely objective knowledge about Jesus that is going to save us. Jesus (or God) is not an object among objects. He alone is the revealing object, that figure who stands above time and space and history and infinity, and he reveals what? He reveals that the Father loves us, that he only loves us, and that if

---

1. Barth, *Church Dogmatics*, 1/1:36.
2. Torrance, *Transformation and Convergence in the Frame of Knowledge*, 263–84.

we come to know the Father as he did we too can have the assurance that we are loved.

One cannot practice theology as something purely intellectual; to try and do so is automatic failure because God is not an object, and because we are so stuck in the bog of our sacrificial religiosity. But we do not give up our brain when we follow our heart, to do so is folly. Rather, we learn to think within the gospel, where all terms are defined in relation to the revelation of God in Jesus Christ crucified. We allow the message to reshape and reconfigure our thinking. And when we do so we engage in theological repentance. We turn from our old, tired gods to the Living and true God. As we walk with Jesus and learn from him how to relate to one another without rivalry and envy, his message about his Father becomes clearer. The bottom line of the good news of the gospel is this: no one ever has to fear a god again, for the true God has demonstrated, in the face of brutality, evil and systemic corrupt hatred and bile, that all are loved, and all are forgiven.

It took the early church several hundred years to codify this in the Nicene Creed. What began as a baptismal formula would become a theological exploration of the divine character. But there was something lacking in the Creed. It has a hole in it that needs to be filled. It lacks history. It is a wonderful metaphysical rendering of the God of the gospel, but the only connection to the historical in it is the reference to Pontius Pilate. In the creed, Jesus is born, suffers, and dies and that is it. There is nothing about his life. One seeks in vain for the words love, grace, mercy, and peace. The God of the Creed is emotionless, apathetic.

When the framers of the creed sought to show that indeed the Son, Jesus, was the same as the Father and not a separate god, they so focused on his divinity that his humanity was ignored. This would cause all kinds of major problems for theological discussions after that in late antiquity, and it is responsible for the gap between history and faith uncovered by early Enlightenment thinkers.

If we have any hope of doing theology as a science, we must begin with the revelation of the gospel about the character of God. We are called to trust that revelation and follow Jesus as we discover the manifold implications of learning to live in love, mercy and peace.

And so, the right side of the chart seeks to conceive of the classic Christian doctrines in terms familiar to us from the left side, or the anthropological side of the chart. My shorthand on the right side of the chart is meant to show how certain theological themes and texts play a role in constructing doctrine. And at the center point of the text is the trinitarian cruciformity. I have a few other items I would add to the chart these days, but it is complicated enough. All I am trying to show is that the very best Christian theology can be retained. We do not need to throw out the baby with the bath water when it comes to understanding and living out our faith. We just need to learn that there is no Christian theology without trusting Jesus and his message about the Father. It all begins here, and it all moves out from here.

Doctrine matters because doctrine is the intellectually linguistic way you communicate why you behave the way you do. Your actions show your faith and your language about God in relation to these matters. One does not create doctrine by stringing together Bible verses and following them. We do not follow a book; we do not imitate a book. We imitate each other as human beings and Jesus is given to us as a model human, indeed the True Human, to imitate. Those whose trust lies in a book will never know the extraordinary peace that comes with knowing the Father.

Furthermore, one cannot jettison the trinitarian revelation and follow Jesus. Jesus is the trinitarian revelation and the trinitarian revelation is Jesus. Those who would deny that God raised Jesus from the dead, and for whom Jesus is merely a good man, a social prophet and Reformer, will not long be able to sustain themselves as they have bought into the "ugly ditch" between history and faith. They will be explorers of all manner of spirituality because they do not walk Jesus's Walk and thus do not participate in his spirituality. They will come up empty handed again and again and turn to other religions for help. Those who trust in human reason will never know the extraordinary peace that comes with knowing the Father. Doctrine matters.

If there is a congruence between the mimetic anthropology and Classic Christian dogmas it is because both stem from reflection on the same set of documents, the Jewish and Apostolic Scriptures, the Bible.

Why has it taken so long for us to understand this? We have been lied to for so long that we are brainwashed. We needed our sacrificial mechanisms to keep our societal peace. The twentieth century witnessed simultaneously the collapse of our sacrificial mechanisms and the revelation of that collapse. World War I was supposed to be The Great War, the war to end all wars. Same with World War II. But World War II brought with it a new knowledge: that we humans are capable of the extermination of an entire religious tradition, and worse, that we developed bombs that could destroy the whole world. Now we are on the verge of Artificial Intelligence, robotics, and potentially World War III.

We keep failing at this thing called humanity, society, culture. Over and over again we try, and over and over again we fail. Christian nations have all failed and Christian nationalism is an oxymoron. Other religions and ideologies have also failed. So why is it that our so-called postmodern period seems to be replete with failure after failure of institutions, religious and secular? How did we end up with such an incredible amount of distrust in society? It is all a result of the gospel bringing to our corporate consciousness that God neither wants nor desires sacrifice of any sort, anytime. It exposes our sacrificial mechanisms as gaudy Bacchanalian orgies of greed, lust and power. It exposes the underlying dynamics of envy, jealousy, and the need to conquer absolutely. The gospel names us for what we are and if we will allow it, it renames us to who we can become when we become like God, the Father of all Light and Love.

Once you see all this you can't unsee it. You will see it live in the interactions of others at church, at the grocery store, on a plane, in your home. You will see it when you read the newspaper or listen to a podcast or watch a movie or listen to music. You will see mimetic displays everywhere, and then it will make sense. You will see anew what the gospel is all about—transforming us from selfish and self-centered to relationship centered and Centered Self. The gospel touches everything in our lives. It affects our thinking, but it also affects us at the deep level of the "soul." It affects the way we live with one another in very concrete ways, and it affects us on psychological levels. The gospel is about the redemption of the whole person, not just some inanimate soul. We were meant to live joyous, wondrous, rapturous lives independent of our circumstances. Our joy comes from knowing that at the end of the day the darkness will be overcome as the Light shines. Our wonder comes from trusting that death does not have the final word, and that that word is life, given by the "Holy Spirit, Lord and Giver of Life." Our rapture comes from learning to live at peace with one another, ourselves and nature.

Our transformation is not something mystical. It is actual, behavioral, tangible. Our transformation has absolutely nothing to do with any set of rules or regulations or even the need for them.

Most spirituality, ethics, and theology are separated in the Christian tradition. I am contending that they are all the same thing expressed in different forms. When what we say about God, how we relate to others, and how our deepest self relates to all things are congruent we will find that life is really not about what we think it is. We discover we are not who we think we are. Our reorientation is so total that prayer and social interaction become one and the same, and both reflect the wonderful gospel we trust in.

There are two key components to apostolic life: *kerygma* and *didache*. *Kerygma* is preaching. It is the message. *Didache* is teaching, the development of the skill sets that constitute authentic Christian living. This book has been about kerygma, about the message that is the gospel of God that we preach. It is the first step, necessary for us to understand before we can learn how we live this day by day. That is what the companion book, co-authored with my friend Keith Hayes, *Liberating the Teaching of Jesus: Christian Discipleship in an Age of Crisis*, will explore.

# Bibliography

Barth, Karl. *Church Dogmatics* 1/1. London: T&T Clark, 1960.
———. *Church Dogmatics* 3/3. London: T&T Clark, 1960.
———. *Church Dogmatics* 4/1. London: T&T Clark, 1960.
Bateson, Gregory. *Steps to an Ecology of the Mind*. Chicago: University of Chicago Press, 2000.
Bonhoeffer, Dietrich. *Letters and Papers from Prison*. Minneapolis: Fortress, 2010.
Ekblad, E. Robert. "God Is Not to Blame: The Servant's Atoning Suffering According to LXX of Isaiah 53." In *Stricken by God?*, edited by Brad Jersak and Michael Hardin, 180–205. Grand Rapids: Eerdmans, 2007.
Garrels, Scott R. *Mimesis and Science*. East Lansing: Michigan State University Press, 2011.
Girard, René. *Things Hidden from the Foundation of the World*. Stanford: Stanford University Press, 1987.
Hardin, Michael, ed. *Reading the Bible with René Girard*. Lancaster: JDL, 2016.
McGrath, Alastair. *The Science of God*. Grand Rapids: Eerdmans, 2004.
Mishra, Pankaj. *Age of Anger: A History of the Present*. New York: Farrar, Straus and Giroux, 2017.
Morris, Stephen. "The Nature of Mimetic Desire: Interdividuation as Phantom Community." Unpublished paper delivered to the Colloquium on Violence and Religion, 2004.
Schweitzer, Albert. *The Quest of the Historical Jesus*. New York, MacMillan, 1968.
Torrance, J. B. "Covenant or Contract?: A Study of the Theological Background of Worship in Seventeenth-Century Scotland." *Scottish Journal of Theology* 23 (1970) 51–76.
Torrance, Thomas. *Transformation and Convergence in the Frame of Knowledge*. Grand Rapids: Eerdmans, 1984.
Wink, Walter. *Engaging the Powers*. Minneapolis: Fortress, 1992.
———. *Naming the Powers*. Minneapolis: Fortress, 1984.
———. *Unmasking the Powers*. Minneapolis: Fortress, 1992.

www.ingramcontent.com/pod-product-compliance
Lightning Source LLC
Chambersburg PA
CBHW031349160426
43196CB00007B/795